MW00450544

The Binge Eating and Emotional Eating Cure

The Secret Code for Eating Disorder Recovery, Never Bingeing Again, and Ending Your Lifelong Struggle With Food Addiction

Alison Tyler

Table of Contents

© Copyright 2018 - All rights reserved.

It is not legal to reproduce, duplicate, or transmit any part of this document in either electronic means or in printed format. Recording of this publication is strictly prohibited and any storage of this document is not allowed unless with written permission from the publisher except for the use of brief quotations in a book review.

Introduction

The one thing that every living thing on our planet has in common is our dependency on food to survive. As human beings, we were meant to have control over food. However, when food takes control over your life, you have a serious issue. If this is your predicament, then this book is here to help you. I understand how it feels to have a never-ending craving for food even after eating. I know what it feels like to hate your body because of excess weight. I know how pleasant it is to turn to food for comfort after having a stressful day. I thought my eating habits were completely okay and I choose to believe that I didn't have a problem.

However, despite my denial, it took my friends and family confronting me for me to finally realize that I had an eating disorder. Food had completely taken over my life- I was distancing myself from my friends and family. After realizing how severe my problem had gotten, my family intervened to show me how much my unhealthy eating habits were affecting me. After that intervention, I woke up with a mission to turn my life around. After hours of research, I stumbled upon various methods that I used to regain control of my life and recover from a lifetime of bad eating habits.

Whom is this book for?

- Anyone who wants to learn how to regain control of his or her life

- Anyone who wants to know the various treatment methods available to treat eating disorders
- Anyone who wants to know how to recognize signs of binge eating and emotional eating
- Anyone who wants to know how to prevent relapses while recovering from an eating disorder
- Anyone who wants to have self-control over food
- Anyone who wants to help their loved ones recognize they have an eating disorder.

However, before we dive into the secrets I discovered that helped me regain control over my life; it is essential for us to discuss the importance of food and eating disorders. Some of these things may seem obvious, but, very few people recognize just how important it is to deeply understand them. These two topics will form the basis of our book and it will help you understand what happens when you lose control over food.

The Importance of Food

Food is an important part of every human's life. It gives your body the nutrients and energy it requires to develop, to grow, to move, to play, be healthy, learn, think, and be active. From the food you eat, your body requires five essential nutrients for it to perform its daily functions. These five essential nutrients are carbohydrates, vitamins, fats, proteins, and minerals. A deficiency in any of the above nutrients can result in health risks that can lead to chronic conditions. Each of these nutrients has specific functions they perform to ensure that you are healthy.

Carbohydrates: Carbohydrates have six major functions; regulating blood glucose and providing energy, dietary fiber, giving flavor, acting as sweeteners, preventing ketosis and breaking down fatty acids, and using proteins sparingly for energy.

The primary role of the carbohydrates you consume is to provide your cells with energy. Most of the cells in your body use glucose as their primary source of energy versus compounds like fatty acids. However, when your carbohydrate intake is above the required amount, you end up distorting the functions of your hormones.

Vitamins and minerals: Your body requires vitamins and minerals in small quantities. They control plenty of processes and functions in your body. Vitamins and minerals are also responsible for building body tissue and your bones. The essential vitamins your body requires include Vitamin A, Vitamin B, Vitamin C, and Vitamin D.

Vitamin A helps in the prevention of infections. It also helps in keeping your eyes healthy. Vitamin A is essential for the proper growth of children. Examples of foods that contain vitamin A include pumpkins, carrots, sweet potatoes, dark green vegetables like spinach, and liver, among others.

Vitamin B helps your body burn nutrients, and this enables the body to release the energy it requires to build and repair worn-out tissues. Other nutrients classified as vitamin B include folate, thiamine, and niacin. Some foods that contain vitamin B are milk, eggs, liver, fish, dark green vegetables, and poultry meat.

Vitamin C enables your body to absorb iron and utilize the nutrients it absorbs to build your blood vessels and bones. Most fruits, especially citrus fruits, as well as vegetables and potatoes are excellent sources of vitamin C.

Vitamin D helps absorb and utilize the calcium to build and strengthen your bones and teeth. Excellent sources of vitamin D are eggs, cheese, milk, fish oils, and liver. Your body can also produce vitamin D by exposing your skin to sunlight.

Important minerals include zinc, iron, iodine, and calcium.

Proteins: Proteins are complex and large molecules, they play a crucial part in your body. Proteins play a significant role in the structure, regulation, and functioning of body organs and tissues. Proteins are comprised of hundreds or thousands of other smaller units known as amino acids. There are twenty types of amino acids and each amino acid has a unique function. Here are a few examples of amino acids and their different functions.

Antibodies: Antibodies help in protecting your body by binding to specific foreign particles like bacteria and viruses.

Enzymes: Enzymes are responsible for a majority of the chemical reactions that take place in your cells. Enzymes also assist in the formation of other molecules and this is done by reading your genetic information.

Structural component: Structural component proteins are responsible for providing support and structure to your cells.

Fats: Fats have several functions which include:

- They are a source of energy: Fats serve as alternative sources of energy. Each gram of fat you consume yields approximately nine calories of energy and this is twice the amount your body acquires from protein and carbohydrate sources. Your excess energy is stored as fat.
- Satiety value: One significant characteristic of fats is that they take time before leaving your stomach. This delay during digestion helps delay hunger pangs and contributes to you feeling fuller after eating.
- They are an excellent source of fatty acids: Your body requires fatty acids, yet it cannot synthesize fatty acids, so the only source is from your diet. These fatty acids are important as they help your body grow and maintain a healthy skin.
- Insulation: Fat deposits beneath your skin function as insulation materials for your

body. It also protects your body against disease.

- Palatability: Fat plays a significant role in the palatability of various foods. It's no secret that high-fat foods tend to be tastier- fat helps food smell better and taste sweeter.

- Body regulator: Fat helps your body regulate the excretion and uptake of nutrients.

However, despite the numerous benefits our bodies receive from food, neglecting to eat a balanced diet can have serious consequences on your health. I'm sure you have heard the phrase "you are what you eat", if you have unhealthy eating habits, you put your body at risk of contracting chronic conditions. Unhealthy eating habits can also lead to an eating disorder.

What is an eating disorder?

An eating disorder is an illness characterized by unhealthy and irregular eating habits and concern or distress about body shape or weight. Eating disorders are some of the most dangerous and difficult addictive conditions to treat. The reason for this is that food addictions are inescapable. You need food to live- you literally can't quit it like smoking or even alcohol. While substance abuse is extremely difficult to recover from you can live without ever seeing drugs again. Eating disorders include excessive or inadequate food intake and this form of unhealthy eating habits leads to extreme damage to an individual's health. No matter which you are dealing with, you will still have to deal with food every day of your life after recovery.

Some of the most common eating disorders among both males and females are Bulimia nervosa, Anorexia nervosa, Binge eating disorder, and emotional eating disorder. In this book, we are going to focus on binge eating disorder and emotional eating disorder. We are going to look at the causes of binge eating and emotional eating. We are also going to discuss the various treatment options available for these eating disorders. We are going to take an in-depth look at the characteristics of each disorder and the effects of binge eating disorder.

This book will also help you identify the warning signs of disordered eating in your loved ones. The earlier you take action and begin the treatment process, either for yourself or someone else, the easier it is to break food addiction.

I hope that the secrets in this book will help you just as much as it did me. Let's dive in.

Chapter One: Understanding Binge Eating And Emotional Eating

A majority of people including myself have had times during holidays or special occasions when we tend to eat too much. However, for some, this is a regular occurrence. They just cannot stop eating even when they are already uncomfortably full. In this chapter, we will take an in-depth look at emotional eating and binge eating. We will also acquire a clear understanding of the definition of binge eating and emotional eating. We will look at the symptoms of each disorder and discuss the differences between emotional eating and binge eating.

Understanding Binge Eating

Binge eating is also known as compulsive overeating. It is the recurrent consumption of food in large quantities usually to the point of discomfort and it is done very quickly. People with binge eating disorder find it hard to stop eating and can't exercise self-control over food. Researcher and psychiatrist Albert Stunkard was the first to explain what binge eating disorder was, in 1949. He explained it as night eating syndrome. The term binge eating was later created to define similar eating behavior without the nighttime aspect.

How Common is Binge Eating?

In the United States alone, binge eating disorder has become one of the most common disorders. Approximately 2% of men and 3.5% of women have binge eating disorders in the United States. Binge eating disorder in men is quite common in midlife, usually between the ages of 45 to 49, while in women it can begin in early childhood, but most often between the ages 18 and 24. Approximately 1.6% of teenagers are affected by binge eating disorder. There is, however, a large number of children and adults who experience episodes of binge eating, but the binge eating episodes are not frequent, which makes it difficult to classify as binge eating.

Key Characteristics of Binge Eating

Some of the key characteristics of binge eating that makes it distinct from other eating disorders include:

- Frequent binge eating episodes, which involve consumption of huge amounts of food over a short time period. The amount of food consumed during a binging episode is more than what most people can eat under similar circumstances.
- Binge episodes are characterized by an overwhelming lack of self-control and the failure to stop indulging in food.

- Binge eating also has a variety of distinguishable eating habits. Some habits include continuously eating when full leading to discomfort, constantly eating even when not hungry, and eating food very quickly.
- After binge eating episodes, a person can experience feelings of shame and guilt about the amount of food they consumed while binge eating, and even the manner in which they ate the food. Binge eating episodes occur at times of boredom, distress, anger, or stress and these episodes could be a way for a person to cope with their emotions.
- People with binge eating disorders have secretive behaviors when it comes to food. They end up eating in secret because they are ashamed and embarrassed about their bingeing sessions.

Signs and symptoms of binge eating

The signs and symptoms of binge eating are displayed physically, psychologically, and behaviorally. The physical signs of binge eating are:

- Not sleeping well and feeling tired
- Feeling constipated, bloated, or acquiring intolerances to food.
- Eating food more rapidly than normal

- Eating huge amounts of food over short time intervals
- Eating food even when full

The psychological signs of binge eating include:

- Increased sensitivity to weight, food, exercise, or body shape comments
- People with a binge eating disorder are majorly preoccupied with their weight, food, and body shape.
- Binge eaters experience low self-esteem, shame, and extreme dissatisfaction about their weight and body appearance.
- Feelings of depression, sadness, guilt, irritability, and anxiety during and after a binging episode.
- Fear of eating food with others or in public

The behavioral signs of binge eating include:

- Hoarding or disappearance of food if you share a kitchen with a binge eater
- Having secretive behaviors relating to food. For instance, hiding food wrappers or food and dodging questions about eating or weight.
- A gradual withdrawal from activities that you may have previously enjoyed.
- Increased isolation
- Erratic behavior like spending too much money on food.
- Frequently dieting

- Developing certain food rituals

The symptoms of binge eating mentioned here are warning signs- you can use them to identify and correct binge eating disorder before it gets out of hand.

Diagnosis of Binge Eating

According to the Diagnostic and Statistical Manual of Mental Disorders (DSM-5), the criteria for diagnosing binge eating disorder are:

- Frequent episodes of binge eating. A binging episode is characterized by eating food within a short period. For instance, eating food every two hours. The amount of food eaten during a binging episode is more than what a majority of people would eat under similar circumstances. A binge episode is also characterized by a lack of self-control over what you eat and eating to the extent of being uncomfortably full.
- Binge eating episodes. Binge eating episodes are associated with the following characteristics

Eating plenty of food at a rapid rate

Constantly eating food even when not hungry

Eating food to the point one gets uncomfortably full

Eating alone due to the embarrassment of the amount of food one eats

Feeling very guilty, depressed, and disgusted with oneself after a binging episode.

- Noticeable distress about binge eating.

Diagnostic Tests and Exams for Binge Eating

If a physician suspects that a person has a binge eating disorder, there are certain tests and examinations he or she may run to check for complications or eliminate further medical complications.

A physical exam: This examination includes measuring your weight and height, checking your nails and skin, examining your vital signs like your temperature, heart rate, or blood pressure, examining your abdomen, and listening to your lungs and heart.

Psychological examination: A mental health provider or a therapist will most likely try to investigate and ask questions about one's eating habits, thoughts, and feelings. They may also ask you to fill in a psychological self-report questionnaire.

Lab Tests: Some tests doctors perform when diagnosing binge eating disorder include complete blood count tests and more specialized tests that help check the protein and electrolytes. The tests also try to find out how one's thyroid, liver, or kidneys are functioning. In some cases, a urinalysis may be performed.

Other tests: A doctor may require you to take an x-ray to evaluate whether you have heart problems. Tests may also be done to help determine the amount of energy your body uses as this will help in planning the nutritional requirements for your body. Electrocardiograms are also used to help in identifying the heart's irregularities.

Based on the test and examination results, your physician is able to come up with a suitable treatment program for you or your loved one.

Common Misconceptions About Binge Eating

Like any other disorder, binge eating has some common misconceptions that make it quite easy to ignore how serious this condition is and how detrimental it can be to one's health. Breaking down common misconceptions about binge eating makes it easy to create proper awareness about binge eating. It also helps you find an appropriate treatment for your loved ones or yourself. Some popular misconceptions about this disorder include:

- Binge eating is not a big deal

It is important to realize like any other eating disorder, binge eating is a serious eating disorder that can cause serious health complications. This condition requires appropriate and timely treatment. Unchecked, it can lead to serious health complications. It can also affect a person's quality of life resulting in psychological issues like anxiety, depression, and strong feelings of low self-esteem. Binge eating disorder can also cause physical risks like high blood pressure, heart disease, and cholesterol issues.

Binge eating disorder affects one's concentration, motivation, energy level, work productivity, attention, and relationships. With all the risks that come with binge eating, discarding the notion that binge eating is not a big deal is quite important.

- Binge eating is similar to overeating

A majority of people use binge eating and overeating interchangeably. However, the truth is that each term has a distinctive meaning. For instance, getting another serving of your favorite dish or eating more biscuits than you planned for the day does not mean you are binge eating. Binge eating disorder exceeds one sitting or one meal. While both binge eating and overeating have the same aspect of eating until one is uncomfortably full, people with a binge eating disorder have no control over their eating and binging episodes happen quite often. Overeating is typically done during one meal, and will happen infrequently.

Another significant difference between overeating and binge eating is that individuals with binge eating disorder are not choosy in the food they consume and they cannot stop consuming food even when they desire to. When people overeat, they are quite selective about the food they eat, often it's a favorite dish or a snack they have been craving. Reaching for that one extra cookie from the jar even when you're full is extremely different from binge eating.

- Binge eating only affects overweight people

Another common misconception about binge eating is that it only affects overweight people. This is not true. Like any other eating disorder, binge eating disorder affects all body types and sizes. Despite one of the signs of binge eating disorder being an intense focus on appearance, shape, and weight, it is distinct from a person's actual weight.

- Eating less is a quick fix for binge eating

The common notion for a majority of people is that binge eating is something that a person can control. This makes people assume that they can resolve binge eating disorder by simply eating less. It is important to realize that binge eating is a complex disorder that cannot be resolved by simply reducing the amount of food one consumes or altering the type of food. The foods that people avoid is usually what they binge on. Avoiding foods increases the likelihood of bingeing or overeating. Therefore, eating less or trying to avoid certain types of foods can lead to an increase in binge episodes. One of the best ways to deal with binge eating is by changing your behavior through guidance from specialists.

- Dieting or weight loss help one stop binge eating

One of the root causes of binge eating disorder is long histories of dieting and weight loss attempts. Dieting or weight loss cannot help you stop binge eating; it actually has a high likelihood of increasing bingeing episodes.

Dieting restricts the consumption of certain food types for a certain period and this helps people with binge eating disorders to have a break. However, restricting a certain type of food leaves your body and brain craving that food. Since diets are unsustainable for long periods, it becomes difficult to stick to the diet rules and this eventually leads to a binging episode.

- People with binge eating disorder only eat high-fat foods

The type of foods an individual binge eats are not restricted to high-fat foods. While people may have cravings for certain types of food, people often end up bingeing on a food they do not even like. The reason for this is due to dieting attempts. Restricting various food groups or specific foods may make you susceptible to eating the type of food you cannot eat while on a diet. Or, you may end up bingeing on the diet food.

- This disorder only affects adults

While a majority of binge eating disorders often starts taking shape during adulthood, the range of people suffering from binge eating disorder is much wider. Binge eating disorder does, in fact, affect close to 1.6% of youth between the ages of 6 to 18. However, at this age binge eating disorder is simply termed as loss of control when eating; this is because the amount of food they eat is not excessive. Loss of control when eating affects approximately 10% of adolescents and children. This problem ultimately increases the risk of depression, anxiety, and eating disorders in the future.

- Binge eating only affects women

Another common misconception about binge eating is that it only affects women. Well, this notion is false, especially for an eating disorder. Binge eating disorder affects both sexes, all races, ages, ethnicities, and sexual orientations.

- There is no treatment for binge eating

A majority of people assume that binge eating has no treatment. Thanks to modern medicine, it has become easier for physicians and therapists to diagnose and treat binge eating disorder. By combining psychotherapy with proper medication, individuals suffering from binge eating disorder can finally have self-control when eating.

Learning the truth about binge eating misconceptions helps ensure that you or your loved ones can differentiate between overeating and binge eating. It also makes it possible for someone to seek medical attention before the problem escalates and becomes a danger to your health.

Understanding Emotional Eating

What is emotional eating?

Emotional eating is simply overeating with the intention of responding to your emotions with food. It is also defined as the use of food as a means to help people deal with their emotions rather than satisfy their hunger. The occasional use of food as a reward or as a celebration is not a bad thing. It, however, becomes a bad thing when eating becomes your main emotional coping mechanism. When your primary instinct when feeling angry, depressed, exhausted, lonely, or bored is to open the refrigerator door to reach for food, that is what we call emotional eating.

Emotional eating makes you get stuck on an unhealthy cycle and it does not actually help you deal with your emotions. Eating your feelings makes you feel good for a while but the emotions come flooding back when triggered. Emotional eating also makes you feel worse than you did before due to the amount of food you may have consumed during one sitting.

The biggest trouble with emotional eating is that one is not able to differentiate between emotional hunger and physical hunger. Differentiating between emotional hunger and physical hunger helps you understand what type of hunger is driving you to pick up that box of cookies.

Emotional hunger vs physical hunger

- Emotional hunger is sudden and urgent. Once it hits you, it makes you feel overwhelmed and it increases your urge to look for food. On the other hand, physical hunger is gradual. The need to eat is not urgent, neither does it demand instant satisfaction; unless you truly have not eaten for a long time.

- Emotional hunger causes specific cravings. When someone is physically hungry, the idea of eating anything sounds okay including healthy meals. Emotional eating causes one to crave sugary foods and junk food to acquire an instant rush. When emotional eaters are suddenly hungry they will feel that they only want to eat pizza and nothing else.

- It becomes impossible to satisfy emotional hunger. The more you eat the more hungry you become and this causes emotional eaters to eat until they are uncomfortably full. On the other hand, physical hunger does not require you to stuff yourself. It becomes easy to tell when you are satisfied and this prevents you from eating even more.

- Emotional hunger can lead to mindless eating. It causes people to eat more than they should without really enjoying what they were eating. However, when eating to satisfy physical hunger, you are always aware of what you eat.

- Emotional hunger can lead to shame, regret, or guilt. Eating due to physical hunger does not leave one feeling ashamed or guilty mainly because you are eating to give your body the nutrients it requires. The guilt that comes from emotional eating is brought about by the fact that you know the food you are consuming is causing more harm than good to your body.

- Emotional hunger does not come from the stomach. Rather than experiencing a pang or a growling stomach, emotional eaters experience their hunger in the form of a craving they cannot get out of their head. Emotional hunger even pushes you to think of the type of food you want to eat in terms of its texture, smell, and taste.

The confusion between emotional hunger and physical hunger can cause one to listen more to their emotional hunger and give in to their cravings.

Signs of Emotional Eating

Recognizing that you are an emotional eater is always the first step of getting the right treatment for this eating disorder. Below are some signs that will help you recognize whether you are an emotional eater.

1. Eating when stressed

From the definition, we determined that emotional eaters always turn to food whenever they are stressed. They end up reaching for food unconsciously often at weird hours of the day to deal with the pressure they experience in their day-to-day life.

2. Eating to forget your emotions

Human emotions are part of life and dealing with them is part of the cycle of life. It becomes a point of concern when someone turns to food when they feel disappointed, sad, lonely, angry, anxious, and bored. This reaction is embedded subconsciously, and it becomes automatic for you to reach for food when experiencing any uncomfortable emotion.

3. Food becomes your only pleasure

Once you begin to seek solace from food, it ends up becoming your only pleasure. This makes you turn to food to look for that soothing effect. For some reason, it becomes difficult for you to explain why a cookie, an ice cream, a bar of chocolate, or any other junk food offers you pleasure and comfort.

4. You lose self-control over food

As I mentioned earlier, emotional hunger drives one to eat even when they are not hungry. You continue to eat and end up not knowing when to stop. Your desire for food and eating takes over your life making it impossible to do anything other than eating. At times, you may find yourself going shopping to purchase a particular food to satisfy a craving even when you are not hungry.

5. You have issues losing weight

Because of the amount of food you eat, it becomes difficult to lose weight. You will usually end up gaining excessive weight when you have this disorder. Losing weight becomes a challenge because you are unable to adhere to the technicalities of weight loss. It becomes extremely difficult to stick to a diet when you have problems denying yourself types of food as well as limiting your intake.

6. You are fascinated with food

One major characteristic of people with an emotional eating disorder is that they are fascinated with food. They love eating. They love their food a lot. If they are not eating, they cannot help thinking about the next piece of chicken they will have. Their world revolves around food and this increases their craving and longing for food.

Food becomes a wonderland that offers joy and satisfaction but it does not reciprocate these feelings. This fascination makes them oblivious of their surroundings and it can become a dangerous addiction.

7. You eat to become happy

Emotional eaters depend on food for their happiness. They acquire their positive emotions from food and eating. They don't think of eating as a necessary activity your body requires to stay alive, like walking, breathing, or drinking water. It is important to note that this feeling is completely different from simply appreciating food. This is purely about eating food to obtain positive feelings and this creates an unhealthy relationship with food.

8. You eat when happy

Don't get me wrong, it is not bad to celebrate your victories and happy moments with food. However, always turning to food whenever you are happy is a clear indication food is a necessary companion when you feel happy.

9. You eat and think of eating even when full

Another sign of emotional eating is eating and thinking of eating even when full. It doesn't matter what you eat, or how much you eat, it's never enough. The satisfaction that comes from eating is always temporary and this prompts emotional eaters to eat more food even when full to get that feeling.

Emotional eaters will obsess over x, y, or z food and cannot wait to eat. They can only think of how satisfied they will be once they eat a particular type of food.

10. You always have random cravings

Emotional eating makes people have random cravings that are quite intense and it becomes extremely difficult to ignore them. You cannot explain the cravings and failure to satisfy them causes you to be unhappy throughout the day.

The above signs can also serve as warning signs that you can use to help yourself or your loved ones before the problem with emotional eating escalates beyond control.

Common Misconceptions About Emotional Eating

Emotional eating disorder is one of the most popular eating disorders in the health and wellness community. Despite the available information about emotional eating, there are still myths concerning this condition making it difficult to identify loved ones with such a problem. Debunking these misconceptions will help you learn the proper facts about emotional eating and deal with the problem head-on.

Some common misconceptions about this eating disorder include:

- Emotional eating has no treatment

One of the most popular misconceptions about emotional eating disorder is that it is incurable. However, this notion is wrong. Emotional eating is, in fact, curable with the right treatment methods. The various treatment methods available for emotional eating not only help you stop food from running your life. It also helps you make peace with food.

- Everyone struggles with the same type of food cravings

Another common misconception about emotional eating is that everyone craves the same food. This type of notion may have driven plenty of people to eat what they crave without thinking of the consequence. They believe this is normal behavior- they think that everyone always overeats their comfort food. But always turning to food for comfort, even if it is a common craving, isn't normal.

Understanding this helps you begin to realize you require help.

- You require willpower and self-discipline to stop overeating

This notion is quite common especially among people who think that emotional eating is a choice rather than a disorder. When it comes to health and fitness, there are two common terms our society loves to use; willpower and self-discipline. The truth is willpower or self-discipline will not help cure emotional eating disorder. Eating is an inborn instinct and willpower cannot control this instinct.

Willpower and self-discipline only help in stopping overeating for a short period. It, however, becomes difficult for emotional eaters to hold back their cravings and this causes them to overeat. Eventually, an emotional eater reverts to their habits.

- Replacing emotional eating disorder with a distraction helps get rid of emotional eating

A majority of experts often suggest acquiring a distraction as one of the ways to break emotional eating habits. The truth is using a distraction is a temporary solution for emotional eating. The only way that distractions can help get rid of emotional eating is when you stop pushing your emotions aside and start dealing with them.

Once you start addressing your emotions and taking care of yourself, you naturally begin to stop using food as a source of comfort. It may take time to accomplish but the end result is worth the hard work and effort you put into the process.

Differences Between Binge Eating and Emotional Eating

Plenty of people assume that binge eating and emotional eating are the same. It also can become quite confusing to know what type of problem you might have when you slowly begin to lose control over food. Clearly defining the differences between binge eating and emotional eating makes it easy for you or your loved ones not to despair or have insecure thoughts about their eating behavior.

Here are key differences between emotional eating and binge eating:

Definition: Emotional eating happens in response to emotions or feelings like stress, disappointment, or anxiety with foods that usually have high-carbohydrates, high-calories, and low nutritional value. Emotional eating is when people turn to food for comfort.

Binge eating is eating large amounts of food over a short period. People with a binge eating disorder eat even when they are uncomfortably full.

Amount of food consumed: The amount of food consumed while on a binging episode is more than what a normal person can eat during one sitting. Individuals suffering from binge eating pay no attention to how full or hungry they are; they simply eat a large volume of food, unlike emotional eating. Individuals suffering from an emotional eating disorder tend to eat small amounts of food as long as they are eating something that makes them feel good.

For instance, eating a row or two of a bar of chocolate is emotional eating but eating the entire bar of chocolate within a short period and including other calories is binge eating. Individuals with an emotional eating disorder consume their comfort food in portions, unlike binge eating episodes.

Planning: Emotional eating is often unplanned simply because the desire to eat arises from an emotional feeling. For instance, when having a bad day, you can opt to look for comfort from a bar of chocolate or a box of cookies. However, this causes over-dependency on food, as people tend to turn to food to look for comfort and deal with their emotions.

Binge eating is often planned. Individuals with a binge eating disorder tend to over-consume calories and eat to the point of becoming uncomfortably full. The food they eat is carefully planned depending on what they prefer to eat. They may have even developed a ritual around food.

Learned habits: Binge eating disorder is a learned habit that escalates with time and this makes it difficult to give up. Emotional state triggers bring about binge eating disorder, which leads to overconsumption of food to forget certain occurrences.

Emotional eating is not a learned habit, but with time, it becomes an almost automatic emotional response for people.

Rapid consumption of food: One of the key characteristics of binge eating is the rapid consumption of food with a complete disregard for how full your stomach is. While emotional eating occurs throughout the day and food is not consumed within one meal sitting.

Despite the differences between emotional eating and binge eating, both conditions are still serious and they require treatment.

If you're enjoying this book so far, I would appreciate it so much if you went to Amazon and left a short review.

Chapter Summary

- Binge eating is also generally known as compulsive overeating. It is the recurrent consumption of food in large quantities usually to the point of discomfort and it is done very quickly.
- Emotional eating is simply overeating with the intention of responding to your emotions with food. It is also defined as the use of food as a means to help people deal with their emotions rather than satisfy their hunger.

- We learned about the signs of each eating disorder and the common misconceptions about each

- The key differences between binge eating and emotional eating lie in their definition, the amount of food consumed during one sitting, and the speed at which the food is consumed.

In the next chapter, you will learn the causes of binge eating and emotional eating.

Chapter Two: Causes Of Binge Eating and Emotional Eating

Now that we have a clear understanding of what binge eating and emotional eating is, we are going to take a closer look at the causes of each disorder. This chapter will help you understand that binge eating disorder and emotional eating disorder is not your fault. It will help you tackle the reasons why you overeat during one sitting or why you turn to food for emotional support. Once you discover why it becomes easier to treat the disorder.

Causes of Binge Eating and Emotional Eating

Like any other eating disorder, the causes of binge eating and emotional eating arise from several factors. These factors are either biological, emotional, environmental, behavioral, family history and genetics, or traumatic occurrences. We are going to break down each factor and look at how each can lead to binge eating.

Emotional Factors

Your emotions are the top reason as to why you binge eat or turn to food for support. It is no secret that we all have our ups and downs, but some people have a hunger or an emptiness that runs deep. People suffering from binge eating disorder have emotional needs that cannot be satisfied by food despite the good feelings they get after eating. Well, it is quite okay to eat food as a pick-me-up or a reward sometimes, however, it becomes a problem when your first instinct is to eat whenever you feel upset, lonely, or stressed. Here is how your emotions cause you to binge eat or turn to food for comfort.

- Sadness

The first instinct for a majority of people when feeling sad is to ignore and numb the pain and this sometimes means reaching for food, especially foods that contain a high-calorie count, sugary foods, and fatty foods. The reason for this is that such foods set off a chemical reaction that causes the release of a feel-good chemical known as serotonin.

Eating foods that are high-carb, fatty, and sugary foods is more than just tasting the food; it serves as a pick-me-up. These types of foods give your brain the stimulating feeling it wanted to help you feel better. However, eating to numb your sadness can also cause feelings of guilt and a lack of self-control over your emotions and the food you consume as well. This can lead to the development of an eating disorder.

- Boredom

Picture this- It is a lazy Saturday afternoon and you have just finished spring-cleaning your home. You are sitting in front of your television trying to relax and catch up on a certain show, and you end up reaching for your jar of cookies. A few minutes later, all the cookies are gone. You might have kept taking cookies without even noticing. When you are bored, your brain is not fully aware of its surroundings or what you do. This can result in you eating extra calories that are not useful to the body. Eating when bored can cause a binge eating disorder.

- Stress

Stress is a norm in our society. From our personal lives, professional lives, to social lives, it becomes quite impossible for people not to be stressed occasionally. Society has come up with different ways to alleviate stress. One solution for a majority of people is food. Studies have shown that stress causes an increase in the intake of calorie-dense foods and sweets. The reason for this is that stress causes your body to release a hormone called cortisol. Cortisol causes your body to increase hunger pangs.

People who suffer from binge eating disorder have higher levels of cortisol than people without binge eating disorder. The higher levels of cortisol increase the desire to eat even when full. The stress relief we acquire from food causes your body to feel less stressed for a short time, but then the stress returns.

- Fear

A majority of us get scared and we still have to navigate through unsafe communities, internal struggles, problematic relationships, and other life problems. We are bombarded with various accounts of death, mishaps, illness, and death. One common way people try to alleviate their fears is through the use of food. Various studies have shown that fear can indeed precipitate eating. People who turn to food to alleviate fear often do so to deny or disconnect from a certain experience.

- When you want to connect with a
previous emotion

Everyone has that moment they like to look back on and recall happy memories or events with their families and friends. These memories are referred to as sticky memories because they are complex and multi-sensory memories of your experiences. You may even distinctly remember the sound, sight, smell, feel, and taste of the food you may have eaten during that event. Your desire to reconnect with a particular memory or event can draw you to eat more of that particular meal to reconnect with the emotions you felt.

Biological Factors

Studies have actually shown that binge eating disorder or emotional eating disorder can actually occur due to biological factors. There is a likelihood for people suffering from an eating disorder to have family members with the same problem. We want to look at how the following biological factors cause binge eating disorder or emotional eating disorder.

- History of dieting

A majority of people suffering from either binge eating disorder or emotional eating disorder have dieted regularly and they may have most probably done it from childhood. Periods of restriction of various foods or calorie restriction often leads to binging episodes. So, what makes dieting a cause of binge eating or emotional eating?

Before we even dive into the issue of how diets cause binge eating or emotional eating disorder it is important to clarify that there are major differences between fad diets and diets that work. The first significant difference is that fad diets market quick ways of losing weight and living healthy lives. Fad diets do not provide your body with enough minerals and vitamins and this makes them ineffective. Fad diets also blacklist certain types of food as "bad foods" and this causes intense cravings while dieting.

On the other hand, diets that work try to create a balance between the foods you eat by providing you with healthy and sustainable changes while dieting. The small adjustments you make are what lead to you losing weight and living healthy after some time. Plenty of people go for fad diets because of their supposed quick results and easy methods. The restrictive, strict, and unsustainable nature of fad diets can leave you feeling hungry all the time.

Dieters can ignore their hunger, but depriving yourself for long will eventually lead to you have powerful food cravings and this will eventually cause you to binge eat. When people suffering from binge eating or emotional eating disorders constantly try to diet, they end up diving deeper into their eating disorder. Fad diets disconnect you from your natural body responses through food restrictions and imposed food rules. It also makes you overlook physical activity, hunger, and your individual nutrition requirements.

Exposing yourself to regular diets will eventually lead to an eating disorder. Other physical effects of repeated dieting include:

- It slows your body metabolism
- It causes you to crave food, and this leads to an increased appetite
- It reduces your total amount of bone density and muscle tissue
- It can cause diarrhea or constipation
- Your body temperature is lowered in order for your body to use less energy
- Repeated dieting reduces your body's ability to tell you when you are full or hungry and this makes you confuse hunger pangs with emotional needs.

Psychological effects of repeated dieting include feeling off due to lack of self-control. It can also lead to obsessive behaviors and thoughts surrounding food. In addition to the above effects, people who diet frequently also have a high likelihood of experiencing depression.

- Genetics

While genetics might seem like a minor cause of an eating disorder, it is, in fact, one of the major causes of binge eating. According to a new research finding published in the Biological Psychiatry Journal, genetic influence is in fact involved in binge eating disorder. In a study conducted at the Boston University School of Medicine, the researchers were able to identify a specific gene in mice that is linked to binge eating. In this particular research study, the scientists were able to discover the link between binge eating disorder and a gene mutation in a gene known as CYFIP2 or the cytoplasmic FMR1-interacting protein 2.

This finding represents the first gene factors to be associated with binge eating disorder. Scientists were also able to discover that the characteristics and behaviors associated with binge eating disorder are likely to be connected to a decrease in the transportation of genes that are required in myelination. Myelination is the process responsible for the formation of the sheath protection found around your nerve fibers. Myelination is a requirement as it allows your nerve impulses to flow quickly across your nerve fibers. These findings could potentially lead to treatment for binge eating disorders by targeting the CYFIP2 gene.

Researchers are also interested in learning whether the normalization of myelination can result in normalized eating behaviors for individuals that suffer from a binge eating disorder.

- Hormone irregularities

One of the major characteristics of binge eating and emotional eating disorders is the loss of control when eating and this can lead to an ingestion of large amounts of food either in one sitting or throughout the day. Eating plenty of food in one sitting or throughout the day affects your hormones, however, hormone irregularities is also a cause of binge eating and emotional eating. Hormones are chemical-like substances found in your body that help in regulating several processes like satiety, food intake, and hunger. Hormones are located in different parts of your body and this makes it easy for them to fulfill their roles in ensuring various processes run smoothly.

Hormones found in your gut like cholecystokinin (CCK), ghrelin, and leptin, influence the rate at which your stomach empties, prompt feelings of hunger, and they also control the amount of food you eat until you are satisfied. Too little or too much of these hormones can cause complications, especially to your eating. We are going to look at how hormone irregularity can cause an eating disorder.

1. Gut hormones

Hormones that are made by the GI system or the gastrointestinal system are also known as peptides or gut hormones. As I mentioned earlier, gut hormones are responsible for controlling the amount you eat and they signal both satiety and hunger to your brain. The gut hormones include:

Leptin: Leptin is a hormone responsible for satiety and is produced by fat cells. The level of the leptin hormones in your body correlates with your body weight and fat mass. This means that an extreme weight loss can actually decrease the levels of leptin and cause a decrease in appetite. While an extreme weight gain can lead to an extreme increase in leptin levels and cause an increase in appetite.

Ghrelin: Ghrelin is secreted by the gastrointestinal cells of your stomach when it is empty. Unlike leptin, ghrelin works in the opposite manner. The stomach excretes ghrelin when it is empty and stops excreting when the stomach is full. Therefore, ghrelin sends signals to your brain to indicate when you are hungry and the hunger pangs steadily increase as mealtime approaches. Ghrelin levels also steadily increase during the day and the levels are highest before dinnertime. This hormone plays two significant roles in balancing your energy. Its first role is signaling your brain, and this causes an acute food intake increase while also increasing gut mobility and speeding gastric emptying.

Its second role is contributing to the experience of eating, especially foods that are high in sugar and fat. Having high or low levels of ghrelin can actually affect your eating behavior negatively. Increased levels of ghrelin can cause a significant shift in the type of food you prefer to consume. The type of food people with high ghrelin levels prefer to eat are energy-dense foods that are high in sugar and fat. An increase in ghrelin levels can also cause the urge to constantly snack to satisfy the hunger pangs you experience throughout the day.

Unlike leptin, ghrelin levels do not depend on your body weight. The increase in ghrelin levels depends on various factors like physical and psychological stress. Physical and psychological stress does actually cause an increase in ghrelin levels and this drives people to eat to satisfy their emotional needs. Thus, the higher the ghrelin levels the more you binge eat or eat food for comfort. High levels of ghrelin also decrease your ability to feel satisfied.

Cholecystokinin (CCK): CCK is a hormone that is produced by both the brain and gut. It reduces appetite, hunger, and gastric emptying. Irregular levels of CCK can cause constant feelings of hunger and this can lead to regular binging episodes. It can also cause you to turn to food for comfort.

Glucagon-like peptide-1 (GLP-1): GLP-1 is a hormone that is released by the lower part of your gut. It slows down the emptying of the gut and causes you to feel satisfied. However, recent research studies have also discovered that GLP-1 also plays a significant role in sending satiety signals to your brain. Irregular levels of GLP-1 can cause binge eating episodes or emotional eating.

2. Sex hormones

Sex hormones are not only crucial for the development and health of your reproduction and sex organs; these hormones also play a significant role in regulating your appetite. The cyclic change of progesterone and estrogen has a significant impact on the risk of binge eating and emotional eating.

Estrogen: Estrogen is a sex hormone made by the ovaries. This hormone is essential for the development of a female's body as well as during ovulation. However, estrogen does indirectly increase the effect and concentration of serotonin in the brain. There is a direct correlation between low serotonin levels and increased binge eating episodes. Women with abnormal levels of estrogen have high tendencies for binge eating due to decreased levels of serotonin in the body.

Progesterone: Progesterone is a female sex hormone produced by the placenta and ovaries. This hormone is necessary as it helps in preparing the uterus for a pregnancy and it sustains the pregnancy as well. According to a few studies, binge eating episodes or emotional eating increases when estrogen levels are low and progesterone levels are high. This typically happens during the menstrual and premenstrual portions of a woman's cycle.

Testosterone:_Testosterone is a sex hormone made by the ovaries in women and by the testes in men. This hormone is associated with the maintenance and development of the secondary sex characteristics of women and men. It is also responsible for the development of lean muscle mass and bones. Studies have found evidence that suggests that increased levels of testosterone are in fact linked with an increase in food intake and appetite levels.

3. Adipokines: Adipokines are cell signaling proteins or cytokines that are secreted by adipose tissue. The primary role of the adipose tissue is to release hormones, which signal the energy balance state of your brain and this helps in regulating your sense of satiety and hunger. Some members of these cell-signaling proteins include leptin, apelin, and chemerin among others. Each of these cell-signaling proteins plays a significant role in controlling your satiety and hunger feelings. An increase in adipokines causes a decrease in satiety and an increase in hunger. This can lead to binge eating episodes. It can also lead to emotional eating especially when under intense pressure.

4. Adiponectin: Adiponectin is a hormone responsible for the regulation of fatty acids and glucose. It also regulates your metabolism and is protective against the development of type 2 diabetes and fatty liver. This hormone is made in the bone marrow as well as in the adipose tissue. A decrease in the level of adiponectin causes a decrease in your blood sugar and this can lead to the development of diabetes. It can also cause binge eating.

There are plenty of other hormones that contribute to energy balance and appetite regulation. An alteration of any of these hormones can result in significant impacts to not only your health but your eating behaviors as well.

- Family History

Studies have found that eating disorders can actually run in the family. These studies suggest that an individual can be susceptible to an eating disorder if a close family member has or had it. This statement does beg the question, "Can eating disorders be inherited?" There is no clear answer as to whether eating disorders like emotional eating or binge eating are hereditary, but some studies do suggest that genetics play a significant role in determining whether eating disorders are hereditary.

According to a study that was conducted to determine the role of genetics in the hereditary aspect of eating disorders, children had a high likelihood of suffering from an eating disorder if their families had a history of eating disorders. The study also looked at the likelihood of individuals having eating disorders like bulimia and anorexia. The results indicate that approximately 56% to 76% of anorexia cases could actually be attributed to hereditary factors.

Apart from the results of the study, there are other reasons why researchers believe that eating disorders are hereditary. One of these reasons has to do with the serotonin receptor gene that is shared among family members with a history of eating disorders. Serotonin is responsible for several behaviors like impulse control, anxiety, and perception. The serotonin receptor gene increases the likelihood of an individual getting an eating disorder like binge eating or emotional eating.

Physical Factors

There is a strong correlation between emotional eating or binge eating disorder and physical factors like body image. We are going to look at how physical factors may cause binge eating and emotional eating.

- Your body image

Your body image is how you see yourself compared to those around you. Thanks to our society, everyone has an ingrained image as to how their body should look. Magazines, social media, and TV shows have contributed a lot to the spread and perception of the perfect weight. Society has created a perfect body image that has plenty of people competing to attain it. However, such unrealistic goals cause many individuals to have a distorted body image and this makes them hate their body.

Distorted body image refers to the unrealistic personal view of your body. This is common for both men and women. In pursuit of that perfect body, people end up having irregular and unhealthy eating habits and this causes eating disorders like emotional eating or binge eating. People start forming their perceptions of beauty, health, functionality, and acceptability from their childhood.

These perceptions continue developing later in life and this creates a negative relationship with your body- this can happen to people of all body types. It may start becoming an obsession and individuals even start envying their friend's body. The more they try to achieve that perfect body, the more they start acquiring irregular and unhealthy eating habits. After years of trying, and never being satisfied with their appearance, they give up and this causes them to use food in extremely unhealthy ways.

How you perceive your body is important. If you respect your body you'll want to preserve it and treat it well. Otherwise, you may end up eating uncontrollably simply because you hate your body.

Social and cultural factors

- Acquired habits

There is no denying that we learn from our surroundings. The same applies to unhealthy eating behaviors that lead to binge eating or emotional eating. As children, what we learn is primarily from our surroundings. Growing up with family members that have an abnormal or negative eating behavior significantly affects how we perceive food and the eating habits we develop as we grow. If your family members had a tendency to turn to food when stressed or happy, then there is a high likelihood that you will do the very same thing when you grow up.

Apart from learning habits from other people, we can also create unhealthy eating habits ourselves that can cause an eating disorder. For instance, when you succeed, instead of rewarding yourself with clothes, shoes, or something of value, you opt to turn to food to reward yourself. Doing this on a regular basis can lead to emotional eating. The more you turn to food as a prize the more your brain registers that food is what makes you feel good. This causes your brain to increase your dopamine levels making you feel even better when eating food. Therefore, acquired habits can actually lead to binge eating or emotional eating.

Other social and cultural factors that cause binge eating or emotional eating include bullying, trauma, weight stigma, and loneliness.

Chapter Summary

- Like any other eating disorder, the causes of binge eating and emotional eating arise from several factors. These factors are either biological, emotional, environmental, behavioral, family history and genetics, or traumatic occurrences.
- The biological factors that cause binge eating and emotional eating include family history, genetics, hormone irregularities, and a history of dieting.
- The physical factors include body image.

In the next chapter, you will learn about the effects of disordered eating.

Chapter Three: Effects Of Disordered Eating

Unhealthy eating behaviors have serious effects on one's health. Learning the effects of disordered eating will help you take action and look for treatment before it causes further complications to your body. In this chapter, we will look at what disordered eating does to your body and the numerous emotional and physical effects that come from binge eating and emotional eating.

What Does Binge Eating and Emotional Eating do to Your Body?

Like any other eating disorder, emotional eating and binge eating are serious issues that people may overlook. Despite people constantly using terms like "eating your feelings," binge eating and emotional eating can actually wreak extreme havoc on your body. The temptation to eat a little more than the required amount of food is always there. When you tend to eat your emotions a lot, or experience binge episodes frequently, it eventually takes a toll on your body. You need to understand what your body goes through when binge eating and emotional eating to know just how severe it can be.

1. Your body experiences increased levels of dopamine

Before we get into how exactly your body experiences increased levels of dopamine, it is essential to understand what dopamine is. Dopamine is a neurotransmitter or a chemical messenger that carries signals from your brain between brain cells. It also helps in controlling the pleasure and reward centers of your brain. In short, dopamine controls the communication between the brain and its cells. Dopamine is a key factor in how we navigate our world.

Everything to do with what makes you feel good, from eating to sex, has a connection to dopamine. Dopamine is responsible for the pleasure you experience when binge eating or eating your emotions. When you eat, your body releases dopamine also known as the "feel good" chemical and this what makes you experience happiness when eating. This feeling makes individuals with emotional eating disorders or binge eating disorder feel great when eating food.

However, since our bodies require healthy foods to control dopamine levels, disordered eating causes an increase of dopamine levels. This is because the fatty foods or sugary treats you usually eat on a binging episode, or while "eating your emotions," cause a release of high dopamine levels. Increased levels of dopamine have serious implications for your body.

One of the effects of increased dopamine levels is an addiction to food. Addiction arises from a flood of dopamine entering the limbic systems in your brain. The limbic system supports various functions like motivation, behavior, emotions, and long-term memory, among others. Once increased levels of dopamine enter your limbic system, it sends a message to your body that you should continue consuming more of what makes you feel good.

Every time you eat a sugary treat or a fatty food, your brain knows what you are eating is making you feel good. Your dopamine levels increase and enter the reward part of the brain. The more dopamine your brain release to your limbic systems, the more you become addicted to food. This is how people with disordered eating end up eating too much food- like with other addictive substances food starts to be the best way to get pleasure.

When you have an increase of dopamine levels in your limbic systems, your brain begins to remove the dopamine receptors to balance the levels. When your brain has fewer receptors, you need to eat more sugary treats to reach the dopamine levels that make you feel good. Fewer dopamine receptors also mean that you become extremely unhappy when you do not get your usual fix of junk food. This causes a withdrawal and tolerance effect for junk food.

Withdrawal and tolerance are hallmarks of addiction. This is the primary reason why an individual with disordered eating always thinks about their next fix of food. Food can even take over their life. It also causes cravings that are quite hard for binge eaters or emotional eaters to ignore and this causes them to eat food even when they are not hungry. This makes binge eating or emotional eating similar to alcohol or drug abuse.

2. Your body immediately experiences physical symptoms

One of the most obvious physical experiences your body immediately has after a bingeing episode is an uncomfortable and overwhelming fullness. This may make you question whether you will have enough room to eat more food later. However, that uncomfortable and overwhelming fullness actually has serious implication for your health. One of the difficult tasks your body tries to perform is trying to balance the amount of food you consume. One of the ways it creates this balance is through digestion.

When your body has an overload of calories from fat and sugar several things happen. First, your parasympathetic nervous system will tell your body to slow down. This helps your body focus on trying to balance the amount of food you consume through digestion.

The parasympathetic nervous system is a part of the nervous system that largely controls automatic processes like your heart rate, digestion, and respiration. It helps your body conserve energy by bringing your bodily functions into homeostasis. Some functions of the parasympathetic nervous system include:

- Regulating your digestion including excretion and urination.
- Regulating your sexual arousal
- It also lowers your blood pressure and slows your heart rate after a flight response is initiated by the sympathetic system.

Once your body slows down to focus on digestion, you start to feel sluggish and tired. As your body continues to digest the food, your pancreatic cells produce insulin.

Insulin is a hormone that enables your body to use the sugar it acquires from the carbohydrates you eat as energy. It also helps the body store sugar as glucose for future purposes. It also regulates the amount of blood sugar in your body- keeping it from becoming too high or too low. Once insulin is released into your body by the pancreas, it leads to the release of serotonin and melatonin hormones.

Serotonin and melatonin are hormones that regulate many human functions such as mood, appetite, and sleep. Serotonin is a neurotransmitter that is responsible for sending brain messages to nerve cells. Melatonin is a neurotransmitter that plays a significant role in your sleeping patterns. This is why you end up becoming drowsy after a bingeing episode. You may also end up struggling to keep your eyes wide open and this is due to an increase of glucose levels from the food you consume.

This interferes with the neurons that produce orexin proteins that are responsible for keeping you alert and awake. Experiencing these changes on a daily basis and often every two hours, surprisingly, causes you to eat more carbohydrates. It also lowers your sexual arousal because of constant regulation of your arousal by the parasympathetic nervous system. The amount of food you eat not only causes a disruption in your sexual life; it also makes you have low energy levels and feel fatigued all the time.

That fatigue happens because your body will focus more of its energy in digesting the food you consume and this depletes the energy you would have used to have a sex life or even be active in other areas of life.

3. You become vulnerable to an unhealthy cycle of dieting and disordered eating

The constant crash of bingeing episodes and emotional eating can make you quite vulnerable to a cycle of dieting and unhealthy eating. One of the common ways people choose to deal with binge eating and emotional eating is through dieting. However, the cycle starts again weeks into your dieting program. The reason for this is that your dopamine levels get low because of the regulation of highly processed sugar and fats. Once your dopamine levels get that low, your body begins to send a mental signal that causes strong cravings, which eventually make you give up dieting.

A majority of people often feel guilty and shameful about cheating while on a diet. The feeling of guilt and shame ultimately makes them turn to food to make them feel better, and the cycle continues. Here are some other reasons why you end up becoming vulnerable to binge eating and emotional eating while on a diet.

- Continuous diet patterns

According to scientific studies, occasional dieting may sometimes lead to compulsive eating disorders in approximately 35% of individuals. The reason for this is that dieting causes your body to experience constant cravings and food obsessions within a few hours into the diet. This easily becomes a root cause for people to stop dieting and enter into a bingeing session. The trick that can help emotional eaters and binge eaters avoid this cycle is to find a diet dictated by your body signals and hunger.

- Forbidden food syndrome

A majority of diets tend to label some foods as "off limit" or "bad foods." The labeling of foods in such a manner tends to make our body obsess over the thing you cannot have. Our human nature tends to obsess and glorify anything that is restricted or termed unfit. According to scientific studies, one of the most long-lasting and common side effects for a majority of people while on a diet is food preoccupation.

Food preoccupation is simply the act of thinking about food even when on a restrictive diet. The more you restrict someone's intake of a specific type of food, the more he/she ends up thinking about it. This often leads to binge eating or emotional eating. This makes it extremely difficult to stick to a diet.

- Final meal frenzy

One of the most common practices for people on a diet is swearing off their favorite snacks or meals. However, not everyone has the self-discipline to stick to this commitment. This leads to a final meal frenzy. Rather than slowly reducing the amount of unhealthy food they eat, people end up getting rid of their favorite unhealthy meals as fast as possible. This quick and drastic change can easily cause emotional eaters and binge eaters to revert to their old habits. Here are some reasons why this can happen:

- Abstaining from and thinking about food for a long period makes it seem ultra-rewarding and extremely exciting. This makes it almost impossible to resist eating it.

- The reward and excitement of the food quickly turn into guilt, shame, and regret. These emotions can make you feel horrible for eating the "bad foods" and getting away with it. This eventually leads to an episode of binge eating mainly because you want to feel better.
- Afterward, we resort to blacklisting food again and swearing that we shall not eat it, and the cycle continues.

Eat and Repent Cycle

As I mentioned earlier forbidding certain types of food and classifying them as "bad" often leads to bingeing sessions or overeating. However, such episodes leave you feeling emotionally hungover and physically crummy. You become defenseless against the overwhelming thoughts that begin to flood your mind. You end up hating yourself for the bingeing session you just had. Once you feel powerless, you end up giving up on dieting.

After a few days, you feel rejuvenated and ready to start your dieting journey again, you end up cheating again, fall back into your old eating habits, and then get back to dieting again. This is what we call the eat and repent cycle. This cycle is extremely unhealthy because your body becomes accustomed to it making it difficult to overcome a compulsive eating disorder.

Remember, dieting is indeed important but when you continuously diet without making much progress, it can have negative effects and increase eating sessions.

4. You lose the natural ability that helps you feel full

One of the most significant changes your body experiences from regular bingeing episodes or emotional eating is losing its natural ability to tell when your stomach is full. Naturally, your stomach was designed to hold approximately 4 liters of volume, which is about 17 cups. However, the feeling of satiety does not come about from when your stomach is full. The feeling of satiety is a result of the brain reacting to the chemicals your body releases when you eat or drink.

It takes the brain approximately 20 minutes for it to register the released chemicals. The delay arises from a disconnection between the food you put into your mouth and the time it takes for the food to get to your gut. When eating, the content levels rise in your stomach constantly for about 10 to 30 minutes. Once your brain sends out signals to indicate that you are full, the stomach can stay full for approximately three to four hours. This helps you continue your day-to-day activities without experiencing hunger.

Once the chemical levels begin to drop, you start feeling hungry again. This is how the body is able to keep you from overeating. However, constantly overeating causes your body to lose its ability to tell you when you should stop eating. Binge eating or emotional eating causes your body to change the levels of essential hormones responsible for helping your brain stop you from eating more food when full. These hormones are in charge of telling you when to put down the fork or pick it up again. The hormones responsible for telling you when to stop eating include:

Ghrelin: As mentioned earlier, but we'll give more detail here, the stomach makes the hormone ghrelin. The major function of this hormone is to stimulate hunger. Ghrelin is able to stimulate hunger by entering your brain and this causes it to act on the neurons present in the hypothalamus. Once ghrelin begins to act on the neurons, the activity in the hunger-inhibiting cells reduce. Once your stomach begins to empty, the ghrelin levels begin to increase and you start feeling hungry. As soon as you fill your stomach with food, the ghrelin levels decrease.

However, compulsive eating disorders cause a constant increase in ghrelin levels and this makes you feel hungry all the time. This is primarily due to the junk food you consume during bingeing sessions. Junk foods, fast foods, and sugary treats are simple carbohydrates. When simple carbohydrates are consumed, they cause your blood sugar levels to spike quickly and drop fast too. This makes you hungry within a short time thus increasing your ghrelin levels.

Cholecystokinin (CCK): The upper small bowel is responsible for the production of cholecystokinin. This hormone helps the brain by giving a sense of fullness once the food reaches the upper small bowel. It also helps in the digestion of food. Cholecystokinin increases the sense of fullness during a meal by affecting the appetite centers of your brain and delaying the emptying of your stomach.

According to several research studies carried out by examining blood levels of cholecystokinin, very obese people appear to have lower levels of cholecystokinin unlike in slim or less obese people. The low levels of the hormone cholecystokinin reduce the sense of fullness and this results in overeating and repetitive bingeing episodes.

Amylin, pancreatic polypeptide, and insulin: The pancreas is responsible for making these hormones. The production of insulin by the pancreas not only helps in regulating blood sugar levels but also in storing excess sugar in the form of glucose. Insulin also helps in inhibiting hunger as it tells the brain when your energy levels are high enough.

Binge eating and emotional eating can cause a breakdown in the production of insulin. A breakdown of insulin production results in increased or decreased levels of blood sugar. It also limits the insulin's ability to send signals to your brain indicating that energy levels are sufficient.

Amylin is a hormone that was discovered in 1981. Its primary function is to inhibit food intake when full. This pancreatic polypeptide is still under study as its role in the body is not yet fully known. There is, however, evidence that the pancreatic polypeptide helps in inhibiting hunger.

Peptide YY, oxyntomodulin, glucagon, and uroguanilin: The last part of your small bowel is responsible for making these hormones. Their major responsibility is to help your body make you full. The release of Peptide YY, oxyntomodulin, glucagon, and uroguanilin happens once the food reaches the gut.

Leptin: Of all the hormones above, the leptin hormone plays a significant role in suppressing your appetite. It was discovered in 1994 by researchers at Rockefeller University. The leptin hormone is made in fat cells. The more the fat cells your body contains, the greater leptin levels your body produces. The primary functions of leptin include regulating your appetite, regulating your food intake, and regulating your weight as well.

Leptin is able to regulate food intake, appetite, and weight through the following mechanisms. First, leptin is able to counteract the effects of the feeding stimulant known as neuropeptide Y. The gut releases this stimulant. Leptin also counteracts the effects of the appetite stimulant known as anandamide. Second, it promotes the creation of an appetite suppressant that helps in notifying your brain when you are full and stops you from eating more food.

However, the leptin can start losing its functioning capabilities due to binge eating and emotional eating. These eating disorders cause a dysfunction in the correct amount of time your body needs to register the number of calories being consumed. This causes the pancreas not to release leptin correctly. Ingestion of food too quickly results in an increased amount of glucose and insulin levels. Once the insulin levels increase, the leptin decreases and this makes it hard for it to counteract appetite and feeding stimulants.

#5. You interfere with your circadian rhythm

Well, I am pretty sure I am not the only one who thinks that sleeping pretty much involves closing your eyes. However, sleeping is much more than that. It involves a natural sequential pattern that helps maintain a proper balance between your active hours and drowsy hours. This sequential pattern is known as your circadian rhythm. A circadian rhythm is like a 24-hour clock system located in your brain's background. This clock helps in cycling between sleepiness and alertness at regular intervals.

Your circadian rhythm affects your mental, physical, and behavioral changes. It also influences your sleep patterns, diet, digestion, hormone release, body temperature, and other necessary bodily functions. However, when your circadian rhythm runs too fast or too slow there can be health consequences. Binge eating and emotional eating are both factors that can cause a disruption in your body's normal circadian rhythm.

The type and quantity of food you eat also play a significant role in your sleeping patterns. When you overeat, your biological clock tends to shift. This shift can cause you to eat even more. The circadian rhythm shift also promotes midnight snacking and it can also cause you to eat even more during the night. Binge eating episodes and emotional eating can also cause you to develop sleep disorders.

How does one develop a sleep disorder from compulsive eating disorders?

First, irregular eating habits like emotional eating or binging episodes confuse your body and this can lead to difficulty falling asleep. The reason you experience difficulty falling asleep while on a full stomach is that your digestive system is working overtime to ensure that the food you have consumed is digested and transformed into energy. The body working and release of energy makes you more awake.

Second, lack of proper nutrition can also disrupt your circadian rhythm causing a sleep disorder. Your body primarily depends on minerals and vitamins to perform different functions. A vitamin and mineral deficiency limits various functions of the body making it hard to reach optimal functionality. This can make it hard for you to fall asleep.

Third, the feeling of guilt, stress, and shame people experience after a binge episode or when eating their emotions can also disrupt your circadian rhythm. These feelings have an impact on the functioning of your body and they play a significant role in the balance of your circadian rhythm. Stress causes your adrenaline glands to kick into high gear. Once this happens, the body tries to counteract this effect by releasing chemicals to balance out the released hormones. This results in a flight or fight response in your body. In this highly active state, it becomes difficult to fall asleep. The problems that come with lack of sleep like drowsiness and irritability makes it easy for people with compulsive eating disorders to snack and find emotional satisfaction in food.

#6. You get heartburns

I hope you do not take the term heartburn literally. Heartburn happens when some of the contents of your stomach are forced back upwards towards your esophagus. This creates a burning pain that is experienced in the lower chest. Heartburns are common problems created by acid reflux. Some major causes of heartburn are obesity, diet, and lack of exercise. The main symptom of a heartburn is the burning sensation experienced in the throat and chest from the stomach acid.

Other symptoms of heartburn include a foul acid-like taste, indigestion-like pain, and a rising sharp pain reaching towards the jaw. Heartburn is a side effect of emotional eating and binge eating. One of the functions of the stomach, apart from digestion, is to produce hydrochloric acid. The hydrochloric acid the stomach produces assists in breaking down food. The more you eat, the more hydrochloric acid your body produces.

The reason your body increases the production of hydrochloric acid is that more food requires plenty of acids to ensure successful digestion. This acid ends up irritating the lining in your stomach and it eventually makes its way towards your esophagus. In the long run, binge eating and emotional eating can cause your body to break down and this can lead to the development of other diseases. An increase in hydrochloric acid can also result in the erosion of the stomach lining resulting in ulcers.

Regular heartburn can also lead the erosion of your esophagus cells and ultimately the development of cancer.

How do Binge Eating and Emotional Eating Cause Heartburns?

One of the common characteristics of binge eating and emotional eating is a large amount of food consumed during one meal or sitting. Eating large meal portions can also cause heartburn. The large amounts of food consumed during a binge episode or when eating your emotions exerts pressure on your lower esophageal sphincter muscle. You find this muscle at the bottom of your esophagus. The lower esophageal sphincter muscle acts like a valve between your stomach and esophagus.

When the lower esophageal sphincter muscle opens, it allows food to go directly into your stomach. Once the food passes into the stomach, the muscle closes to prevent stomach acid and food from flowing back into your esophagus. The pressure that large amounts of food exert on the lower esophageal sphincter muscles causes it to relax abnormally and weaken. This results in stomach acid flowing backward into your esophagus, creating heartburn.

Apart from weakening your lower esophageal sphincter muscle, large portions of food eaten in one serving can also cause your stomach to expand from the pressure the food exerts on your LES muscle. Since your stomach is approximately the size of your fist, the expansion of your stomach causes the LES muscle to open and it allows hydrochloric acid to flow into your esophagus. One of the ways of minimizing heartburns is through reducing the portion of food you consume. However, for someone with an eating disorder, tackling the issues behind the disorder helps in ultimately reducing food portion sizes.

#7. You begin to experience fatigue

Have you ever wondered why you tend to get sluggish and tired when you overeat? Well, the reason for this is simple; the fatigue you experience after you overeat is your body's response to the chemical changes during the digestion process. Experiencing fatigue is common for almost everyone. It, however, becomes an issue when you constantly feel fatigued every time you eat. Experiencing fatigue every time you eat can obstruct you from performing regular everyday activities.

Healthy eating habits do not only lead to a healthy life but also help you remain active throughout the day. There is a direct relationship between fatigue and food. Your body requires an adequate amount of nutrients for it to function appropriately. This is very similar to how a car requires gasoline to function. Without gasoline, a car cannot move. The same analogy applies to your body; without the nutrients it requires, it becomes difficult for your body to function.

Without a constant supply of sufficient calories and nutrients, your body becomes tired and sluggish on a daily basis. This results in you feeling like you have run out of gas to perform your day-to-day functions. The reason why you feel tired and sluggish is due to the overproduction of insulin. An insulin level spike often leads to your cells becoming resistant to the effects of the insulin spike. Therefore, the more you binge eat, the more your body overproduces insulin and this results in low blood sugar and cell resistance to the effects of insulin.

Binge eating and emotional eating can also create an unfortunate cycle that causes your pancreas to overproduce insulin. The insulin produced is used to process the excess sugar in your body due to binge eating episodes or emotional eating. Your pancreas will not stop producing insulin until your brain indicates that the blood sugar levels in your body are safe.

By the time your brain indicates that the sugar levels in your body are safe, blood sugar levels are extremely low. A low blood sugar level leads to you feeling tired, nauseous, dizzy, and sometimes depressed. To avoid feeling sluggish or fatigued, it important for you to realize how detrimental your unhealthy eating habits are towards your health. The excellent news is that dealing with fatigue can be addressed by eating well-balanced foods and snacking on foods that contain sufficient calories to keep your body well adjusted.

Simply eating to comfort yourself or to keep off hunger is not sufficient. Also, keep in mind, that if you eat too many calories your body will still experience fatigue; therefore, you must strive to eat just the right amount of calories. This is why it is important for individuals suffering from binge eating disorder or emotional eating disorder, to seek treatment. Seeking treatment enables you to deal with your unhealthy eating habits and adopt healthy ones. It will be possible for you to include healthy meals and a good eating schedule as part of your lifestyle.

Physiological effects of disordered eating

1. Obesity and weight gain

Obesity is a chronic medical condition that has a negative effect on your body as well as its systems. Obesity and weight gain is the most significant effect of binge eating or emotional eating. According to statistics, approximately two-thirds of individuals with a compulsive eating disorder are overweight. Binge eating and emotional eating increases the amount of fat in your body. The excess fat present in your body is what is used to define whether you are obese or overweight.

Your body requires a certain amount of fat to perform functions like heat insulation, storing energy, and shock absorption. However, when the amount of fat in your body surpasses the required amount it needs, it ends up becoming excess fat. One of the ways of determining obesity is through body mass index (BMI). Your body mass index offers an approximate indication as to whether you are obese, overweight, underweight, or average. BMI is calculated by dividing your weight in kilograms by your height in meters squared.

Binge eating causes you to overeat and this leads to you putting on extra kilograms within a short time. And since people with eating disorders do not exercise, their weight increases to the point of immobility. Individuals suffering from binge eating or emotional eating disorders often have self-esteem issues because of their weight. Low self-esteem often leads to more eating and this accelerates the problem further.

Excessive weight gain or obesity also increases the chances of you acquiring other diseases and this eventually poses as a risk to your health. Some of the long-term health problems that arise from obesity and excessive weight gain are:

Diabetes: Obesity and excessive weight gain are among the major leading causes of type 2 diabetes. Irregular insulin levels characterize type 2 diabetes. This type of diabetes used to mainly affect adults, it has, however, started occurring in children. Obesity causes a resistance to insulin. Insulin is the hormone responsible for regulating blood sugar. Once your body becomes resistant to insulin, your blood sugar elevates or decreases dramatically.

Heart disease: The condition atherosclerosis, which is the hardening of your arteries, occurs more in people with obesity than in individuals who are not obese. Obesity causes a buildup of fatty deposits in arteries responsible for the supply of blood to your heart. This buildup of fatty deposits causes coronary heart disease. Obesity also causes a reduction in blood flow due to the narrowing of the arteries and this can cause a heart attack or chest pains.

Joint problems: One common aspect of obesity is that it can restrict your mobility and cause joint pains. Due to the extra weight placed on your body, obesity can affect your hips and knees. In extreme cases, the extra weight can make it impossible for obese people to walk. Some cases of obesity may also lead to joint damage.

Metabolic syndrome: According to the National Cholesterol Education Program, metabolic syndrome is a risk factor for cardiovascular diseases. Metabolic syndrome is comprised of six primary components including insulin resistance, elevated blood pressure, abdominal obesity, elevation of some blood clotting factors, and an elevation of specific blood components.

Sleep apnea: Sleep apnea is a respiratory condition that prevents people from breathing for short periods while asleep. This condition interrupts your sleep. Once your sleep is interrupted, you end up becoming sleepy during the day. Sleep apnea also causes snoring. Respiratory problems that are linked to obesity occur because the excessive weight adds weight on your chest and this can restrict breathing.

Cancer: According to several studies, obesity is one of the major contributing factors of cancer among overweight women. Obesity has led to an increase in cancers like breast cancer, gallbladder, uterus, and colon. Obese men are also at a higher risk of suffering from prostate cancer and colon cancer.

Psychological effects: In a social culture where the ideal picture of beauty is that you have to be slim and fit, obese individuals can experience self-esteem issues due to their weight. The weight of obese individuals can also affect their ability to perform day-to-day activities. This causes them to be socially isolated.

Finding a solution for obesity when you have an eating disorder starts with you acknowledging the reasons why you binge or emotionally eat. Once you identify these reasons, you can take the next step to lose the excessive weight. Consult a dietician to help you come up with an exercise and diet routine program that will help you lose weight. The more you can understand what triggers your eating disorder the better treatment plan you can put together.

2. Gastronomical issues

One of the most affected areas of your body due to binge eating or emotional eating is your digestion system. Let us look at the effects the volume of food you eat has on your digestion. We will start from your mouth and break down how binge eating and emotional eating affects your organs.

Step 1: When the food goes in

When the food gets to your stomach, it stretches because of the amount of food you ate during one sitting. Your stomach is elastic, it has the ability to stretch to accommodate the amount of food consumed by you every day. Therefore, when you eat a large amount of food during a binging episode, the first thing your stomach does to accommodate the food is stretch. However, since emotional eating and binge eating disorders happen on a regular basis, your stomach stretches permanently. The bigger your stomach gets, the more food it is able to accommodate. This causes you to increase your food intake, and it escalates the eating disorder.

Another effect of regular binging episodes is that it causes your stomach to send your brain mixed signals about your satiety level. The neurological tissue responsible for signaling your brain that your stomach is full begins to malfunction and it becomes difficult for the brain to tell whether you are full or not. This becomes dangerous since you can continue eating without realizing whether you are full or not.

Step 2: A failing stomach can cause the pancreas to go into an overdrive

Binge eating or emotional eating on a regular basis can have unfortunate consequences on your pancreas. Consuming an excess amount of food on a regular basis causes a dramatic effect on the functionality of your pancreas. Binge eating causes your pancreas to go into an overdrive production of insulin. The overproduction of insulin is due to the large sugar load in your bloodstream which needs to be removed. Your pancreas will not stop producing insulin until your brain indicates that the blood sugar levels are safe. However, by the time the brain sends your pancreas a signal that the blood sugar levels are safe, your blood sugar is already low, and this can cause effects like dizziness, tiredness, and even depression.

Step 3: An excess amount of calories causes a fatty liver

Binge eating on a regular basis causes your liver to overwork and this causes your liver to store excess fat. How is this possible? The primary function of your liver is to prevent a decline in your blood sugar while the function of your pancreas is to prevent an increase in your blood sugar. When you consume a large amount of food during a bingeing episode that your body is not capable of burning, the liver ends up storing the excess calories. When the liver cells start storing fat, your liver becomes insulin-resistant and inflamed.

3. Heart disease

A majority of the people who suffer from a binge eating disorder or emotional eating disorder are overweight. Being overweight causes even more health complications. One of the most significant health complications is the risk of a heart disease. The relationship between heart failure and obesity is a complicated one. Obesity is intertwined with other health conditions. Some health conditions that intertwine with obesity are cardiovascular diseases including diabetes, high blood pressure, and an abnormal level of cholesterol. However, the excess addition of fat around the heart can have a direct effect and impact on the functioning and structure of the heart.

The more weight you add, the more the effects your heart experiences. The first effect of excessive weight gain due to unhealthy eating habits is that your heart has to work harder to supply oxygen to your entire body. Another consequence of excessive weight gain is that fat starts to accumulate inside the arteries of your heart. The more you gain weight, the more fat continues to accumulate inside the arteries. This, in turn, causes your arteries to harden.

Thick artery walls cause your heart to pump blood faster since there is not much space for the blood to flow.

Thick artery walls lead to a disease called Atherosclerosis. Atherosclerosis is 10 times more likely to occur in people who are obese than in people who are healthy. Being overweight can also cause future heart failure or a heart attack if fat continues to accumulate around the heart.

4. Type 2 diabetes

People who use food for their emotional health or binge eat have higher likelihoods of developing type 2 diabetes. Diabetes is a lifetime disease, and it requires ongoing treatment. It is common knowledge that the consumption of excess amounts of sugary and fatty foods on a regular basis causes your blood sugar to rise beyond manageable amounts. An increased amount of blood sugar is bad for your health as it can cause your cells to become resistant to insulin. This can lead to type 2 diabetes.

What causes diabetes?

As I mentioned earlier, your pancreas is responsible for the production of a hormone known as insulin. The primary function of insulin is regulating the amount of sugar in your bloodstream and helping your cells turn the glucose it obtains from food into energy. People who suffer from type 2 diabetes have insulin but the cells are not able to use insulin as they should. This is called insulin resistance. At first, your pancreas produces more insulin to keep up with blood sugar levels in your bloodstream. But eventually, your pancreas cannot keep up with the overproduction of insulin and this causes your blood sugar levels to build-up.

Binge eating and emotional eating cause your pancreas to malfunction because of the excess amount of food you consume. Apart from a malfunctioning pancreas, eating disorders like binge eating also cause bad communication between your cells. Communication issues between your cells cause other problems, which eventually lead to diabetes.

Common symptoms of type-2 diabetes

- Being extremely thirsty
- Blurry vision
- Numbness or a tingly feeling in your feet and hands
- Being irritable
- Feeling worn out
- Wounds that take time to heal.

One of the ways to fend off diabetes is through adopting stable eating habits that will eventually lead to a healthier you.

Psychological effects of disordered eating

The relationship between food and your emotions

The reason why binge eating and emotional eating feels good is that there is a direct relationship between your emotions and food. What you eat not only affects how you look but how you feel as well. Also how you feel does dictate what you eat. Hundreds of scientific studies have established that there is indeed a link between food and emotions. A majority of these research studies shows that cravings, stress, irritability, or anxiety do actually result from unhealthy eating behaviors. Understanding the relationship between food and your emotions will help you comprehend the physiological effects of binge eating and emotional eating.

How does food affect your mood?

It is essential to realize that food does affect and influence your mood in a significant way. Food is not only of importance to us for our survival; it also provides your body with essential nutrients required to regulate your physical conditions, mood, and mental conditions. The primary reason why people may use food for comfort is that food has a direct relationship to how you feel. Here is how some foods boost your mood.

- Proteins: Proteins are excellent mood boosters as they help your body increase the release of norepinephrine and dopamine. Proteins also slow down the absorption of carbohydrates into the bloodstream causing an improvement in energy levels several hours after you eat. The various neurotransmitters responsible for improving your mood are made from amino acids, which are present in proteins.
- Vitamins: Despite the variety of vitamins available from different types of food, only a few of them help in boosting your mood. Examples of vitamins that help in boosting your mood include Vitamin D, Folate, and Vitamin B-12. Vitamin D helps

in relieving mood disorders. One of the best ways to access vitamin D is through sunlight. You can also acquire a daily dose of vitamin D from foods like soy milk, egg yolks, or take a Vitamin D supplement pill.

- Vitamin B-12 and Folate also help in easing depression. Some foods that contain folate include broccoli, lentils, and oatmeal. While foods that contain vitamin B-12 are salmon, cottage cheese, and leafy greens.
- Fiber: Foods that have soluble fiber like complex carbohydrates slow down the body's ability to absorb sugar into the bloodstream. Slowing down the absorption of sugar into the bloodstream causes an increase of the hormone "serotonin." Serotonin is a feel-good hormone responsible for decreasing mood swings. Examples of foods that contain fiber include beans, peas, oats, and pears among others.

The above examples of food clearly show that there is a direct relationship between your state of mind and food. Therefore, when you have unhealthy eating habits, the food you eat has a negative effect on your health and mood as well. Here are different ways in which food affects your mood.

1. Depression and Unhealthy eating habits

One of the most common effects of unhealthy eating habits is the repeated occurrence of depression. Recent studies have found that there is a direct relationship between eating disorders and depression. Scientists are constantly finding that when it comes to depression, your mind and food have an intimate link, even more than what was previously assumed. Binge eating and emotional eating causes an individual to eat foods that are high in sugar and fat.

Foods that contain a huge concentration of fat and sugar contribute directly to emotional and biological states that cause depression. When eating poorly, your body interprets the lack of nutrients as a consequence of a disease. In response, your body releases proteins to combat the disease and this can cause inflammation. Another response of your body to the shortage of nutrients is the imbalance of brain chemicals. Unhealthy eating habits cause an imbalance of brain chemicals due to the lack of nutrients.

Studies have shown that diets rich in whole foods reduce the risk of depression while diets that mainly contain processed foods can increase the risk of depression. The reason for this is that whole foods contain natural nutrients with no additives while processed foods have additives and their nutritional value is lost through alterations or processing. The loss of nutrients in processed foods is among the causes of depression.

Other studies that suggest the dangers of unhealthy eating habits are:

- The American Journal of Psychiatry published a study that compared whole foods, whole grains, and fish with a diet comprised of fast foods and processed grains and meat. People who consumed the whole food diet had a lower risk of becoming depressed, unlike people who consumed the diet with highly processed foods.

- A study published in The British Journal of Psychiatry also compared a diet rich in fruits, fish, and vegetables and another diet made up of sweet desserts, fried foods, processed grains, and processed meat. The researchers in this study concluded that eating diets that majorly comprise of processed foods increased the risk of depression with time while eating whole foods reduced the risk of depression.

Each of the above studies proves that unhealthy eating habits do indeed cause depression. With the number of unhealthy foods eaten by individuals suffering from binge eating and emotional eating disorders, depression is a common occurrence for these individuals.

2. The stress connection

Another effect of binge eating or emotional eating is stress. Stress is both a cause and effect of bingeing and emotional eating. It is quite common for people with an eating disorder to turn to food when they are angry, sad, disappointed, or overwhelmed by emotions rather than turn to someone for help.

Turning to food for comfort leads to a cycle that is hard to break. The cycle goes like this: eating when stressed and the feeling bad about eating all that food during one meal and getting stressed about it then eating again.

If your emotions are not dealt with in the right way, it becomes quite difficult for you to break this cycle. The more you binge, the more stressed you become.

3. Social isolation

Social isolation is also a common effect of binge eating and emotional eating. Individuals suffering from these disorders tend to isolate themselves, here are some reasons why:

They tend to compare themselves with others: Weight gain is among the symptoms of binge eating. The excessive weight gain causes people suffering from emotional disorders to compare themselves to people they regard as more fit. You think you look horrible compared to the people around you. This may make a person shut down, they don't want others to see them in what they think is an ugly state, so they stay away from other people.

They are afraid what others will think of the amount of food they eat: Another reason why people suffering from binge eating disorder or emotional eating disorder tend to isolate themselves is the fear of people looking at them differently when they see the amount of food they eat at one sitting. This causes them to push people further and further away. It also makes them eat by themselves and even sneak food to their rooms to avoid being questioned about the amount of food they are eating.

They are afraid they are not good looking: Another common fear for people with an eating disorder is that they do not look beautiful. Thanks to our modern society, many believe that the only way to fit the beauty standards of society is by being thin. The thinner you are the sexier you feel. Well, this perception causes a majority of people to feel uncomfortable in their own skin, body shape, and size. This will result in even more disordered eating.

Unlike other effects, social isolation is dangerous as people end up pushing away their support system and this can cause your eating disorder to escalate. It also causes people to feel worthless, and it increases the likelihood of depression. Once, you start reconnecting with society, you can start recovering and slowly accepting your body and weight.

People suffering from an eating disorder require social interaction as it offers support for them to recover and start adopting healthy eating habits. It also makes you stop being afraid to share your emotions and live life to the fullest. Placing yourself in a cocoon is dangerous, it can cause you to feel lonely, sometimes to the point of feeling suicidal.

While treating an eating disorder, you should strive to come out of social isolation and start interacting with others, even if you need to get help on how to do this. Your therapist will try to ensure that you establish a productive connection with people. The more you connect, the easier it becomes for you to get comfortable around people. Treatment also enables you to start bringing family members back into your life and this makes it easy for you to recover from an eating disorder. With the help of family and friends, you are able to navigate through the difficulties that lie on your path to recovery.

Chapter Summary

- Unhealthy eating behaviors have serious effects on one's health. The effects of binge eating and emotional eating are experienced both physically and psychologically. These effects lead to the development of chronic conditions.
- Some physical effects of disordered eating include obesity, gastronomical issues, and heart disease.
- Psychological effects of disordered eating include depression, stress, anxiety, and social isolation.

In the next chapter, you will learn how to treat binge eating and emotional eating and stop it for good.

Chapter Four: Treating Binge Eating and Emotional Eating to Stop for Good

Now that you know about the causes and consequences of binge eating and emotional eating, let's get to the meat of this book: how to stop and stop permanently. While not all of these tips will work for you, there are many that will, and they will be more effective if you use them together.

You may want to use some of these suggestions at the start of your program to stop binge eating, and save others for later once you get going, or after you hit a roadblock. Changing habits is a dynamic process. If one idea doesn't work, you don't have to keep using it- simply move on to something else. The key is to find what works for you and make it your own.

Stop Dieting

Recent studies show that dieting can actually make it harder to get over a binge eating or emotional eating problem. In fact, dieting can be a trigger for eating disorders in the first place.

The relationship between dieting and eating disorders is complex, and every person's situation is unique. However, think about it from practical terms. If you're struggling to think healthily about food and your body image (or other personal issues like self-esteem), it doesn't make sense to go on a restrictive eating regimen that limits calories or certain food groups.

For binge eaters who do not need to lose weight, dieting could lead to anorexia nervosa, a disorder in which food is strictly limited and an unhealthy amount of weight is lost, leading to dangerous and even fatal consequences. If you are overweight and a binge or emotional eater, simply eating normally again may help your weight return to a healthy level.

Once you get your binge eating habits worked out and maintain healthy eating for a while, you can always see a doctor or other professional (see below) to consult about further weight reduction. It's possible to find, though, that eating healthily, boosting your self-confidence, dealing with emotions appropriately, and practicing mindfulness will make dieting completely unnecessary.

Don't Skip Meals or Go Hungry

Even without an eating disorder, most people don't do well when they miss meals. When you feel like your starving, you're much more likely to overeat when you finally get food in front of you- think about that bread basket on a restaurant table.

Letting yourself go too long without eating messes up all kinds of delicate systems in your body. You lose the ability to receive normal hunger cues, and your blood sugar gets out of whack. You become cranky and fuzzy headed, which also keeps you from eating appropriately when your food arrives.

It's better to eat three, or even four or five, meals per day, depending on your schedule and culture. Of course, you don't want to eat five full-sized meals, but a normal breakfast followed by a smaller lunch and dinner, with snacks in between, is fine. Or you can eat tapas-sized meals throughout the day. Just don't go so long between eating that you gorge when you finally do sit down for a meal.

Clean Out Your Kitchen

Be honest: do you have foods you shouldn't in your fridge or pantry? Foods that you know trigger a binge? At least for now, it's better to get them out of the house.

Think about it. If you have to get dressed, drive to the store, and shop for foods before you can binge eat, it's less likely you'll give in to cravings. Having a healthy kitchen gives your willpower a boost.

Grab a trash can or a big plastic bag and get rid of any opened "no-no" foods. If you have unopened food you don't want to have around, give it to your neighbors, take it to the office, donate it to a food bank, or send it with the kids to school.

If you have other people in the household who will still want to eat your trigger foods, talk to them about at least whittling down the list, so you have a minimum of temptations nearby. It will be healthier for them too. You don't want your kids to grow up with eating problems or your partner to have cardiovascular disease, right?

Start a Mindfulness Practice

Mindfulness simply means thinking about what you are doing in the moment, not distracting yourself with television, pining for the past, or daydreaming about the future. While, of course, mindfulness will assist you with not eating without thinking (like mindlessly snacking in front of the computer screen), it will also really help you not to binge eat or eat emotionally. If you can practice mindfulness not just about food but about all aspects of your life you will be healthier all around.

Having a mindfulness practice as much as possible all day, every day, can do more than make you conscious of your eating habits. Mindfulness can help you recognize, for example, other undesirable behaviors or thoughts that may ultimately lead to disordered eating, such as:

- People pleasing.
- Feeling "less than."
- Comparing yourself to others.
- Being bored.
- Feeling angry or depressed.
- Experiencing anxiety or nervousness.
- Planning poorly.
- Engaging in other addictive behaviors, like shopping, gaming, drinking, etc.

Moment-by-moment, as you go through your day, mindfulness asks you to check in with yourself. "Am I feeling anxious?" If you are, you can counter that emotion with a statement like, "Everything is okay right now; there is nothing to be fearful or worried about."

Gradually, as you begin to recognize times when you are feeling negative or out of control, and give yourself these mini pep talks, you train your brain to calm down and to react to the moment, not at what you fear for the future or to something that happened in the past.

Engage in Moderate Exercise

If you have an excess weight issue as a result of your binge eating (or perhaps as a cause of disordered eating), it can be tempting to think exercise is an easy fix. But for many binge eaters, exercise is another binge cycle, an analog to vomiting.

Until you get your eating habits under control, stay away from heavy exercise. You can always ramp up your workouts a few months after you've begun your treatment or when your eating is more stable.

Use light exercise, like walking or ballroom dancing, to keep your blood flowing and your muscles working. Heavy exercise might just throw you back into a bingeing habit, especially if it leaves you really hungry or too tired to make good decisions after a workout.

Try Yoga or Tai Chi

Another great option for moderate exercise is yoga or tai chi. Not only will these help you maintain strength and flexibility, but they'll also improve your mindfulness because they require constant concentration.

Yoga and "soft" martial arts like tai chi also help heal the body through motions and poses that stimulate blood flow to the organs and open up your posture. You may find yourself naturally in a better mood and less likely to binge when you try these activities.

If you're embarrassed or shy about doing yoga or tai chi in a class, try using a DVD or streaming lessons. You could also hire a private instructor until you get the hang of it or arrange a small group class with friends. There are even therapy centers that offer "Yoga for Eating Disorders" classes.

Get Sufficient Sleep

Did you know that excess weight and inadequate sleep are linked? Lack of sleep may make you too tired to exercise, so your calories consumed wind up exceeding your calories burned. But it's likely there are hormonal associations between too little sleep and obesity too, according to a new area of research.

Certainly, insufficient sleep will leave you groggy and cranky the next day, which doesn't make it easy to resist binge eating or eating in response to emotions. And you're likely to be too tired to prepare healthy meals or make good choices about healthy foods over junk.

If you find yourself lacking in sleep, there can be many reasons for it:

- Not going to bed early enough for your rising time.
- Having to work extremely early in the morning, so it's not practical to go to bed in time to get enough shuteye.
- Excess snoring, or sleep apnea, where you actually stop breathing multiple times during the night (or a partner with snoring or sleep apnea problems).
- Nervousness or anxiety that keeps your mind spinning and your adrenaline pumping.
- Exercising too close to bedtime.
- Consuming too much caffeine, especially afternoon.
- Excess alcohol consumption (alcohol initially makes you sleepy, but then it wears off and can make you wake in the middle of the night).
- Acid reflux (heartburn).
- Eating large meals too close to bedtime.
- Noises that keeps you up or wakes you up (neighbors, dogs barking, traffic, etc.).
- Parenting young children.
- Medication that causes wakefulness.
- Overstimulation (e.g. looking at phones or computers right before bed) or poor bedtime routine.

Join a Support Group

There are all kinds of support groups for eating disorders, and you can find one with the level of organization and participation you need for your unique situation. For example, if you want a more formal group, possibly led by a healthcare provider or therapist, ask your doctor or closest healthcare facility.

If a more informal support group is what you're looking for, you could try a recognized organization like Overeaters Anonymous (https://oa.org/). This group offers local meetings, which you can find by looking online, as well as newsletters, podcasts, and other support materials, so you can do a little research on your own. Overeaters Anonymous (sometimes just called "OA") has resources to deal with all kinds of eating disorders, including binge eating and emotional eating.

Some people just can't make it to a live meeting due to work commitments or childcare. Or they may feel embarrassed about their weight and psychological issues. In that case, anonymous online support groups can be an ideal alternative. You're sure to find people you can talk to on sites like Mumsnet or Reddit.

There are also hotlines (https://www.nationaleatingdisorders.org/help-support/contact-helpline) for those people with eating disorders who feel like they need emergency help. Using your phone, or instant messaging, you can talk to people who can help you get back on track if you're tempted to overeat or get advice about whether you should talk to a healthcare professional. If you think you have a health emergency because of your eating disorder, never hesitate

to dial 911 or have someone drive you to the closest
emergency room. It's always better to be safe than sorry.

Watch Alcohol Consumption

Have you ever had a drink or two and then thrown
caution to the wind, eating an entire carton of ice cream or
a bag of chips? You're not alone. If you are trying to
control binge eating, it's wise to watch your alcohol
consumption at the same time. You don't want to undo
months of hard work with a couple of cocktails.

Decide before a meal or event how much alcohol you
plan to drink, and make sure it won't make you tipsy
enough to start bingeing. Stay away from drinks that make
you get drunk quickly. Pace yourself when drinking,
inserting a mineral water or juice between drinks.

Likewise, marijuana can be a hunger stimulant,
making you eat more. In fact, getting "the munchies" after
smoking a joint could make you fall off the wagon
completely and have a worse effect than alcohol. Try to
avoid all recreational drugs if you're a binge eater.

Stay Hydrated

There are so many benefits to drinking enough water,
but if you're trying to forestall a binge, staying hydrated
may help. Sometimes you think you're hungry, but what
you really need is a glass of water. If you want to eat,

especially if you've just eaten, try drinking a glass or two of water first. It will fill you up, so you eat less, and whatever you eat will be digested more easily.

You can use a tumbler of water to make smaller portions feel like more too. For example, instead of eating a circus-size tub of popcorn, make a small bowl and drink a big mason jar of flavored water with it. You'll be so satisfied you won't even miss the extra snack servings.

Eat to Stay Full Longer

The quality of your food can change too, in order to help you feel full longer. Carbohydrates can be processed really quickly, especially refined ones, so whenever possible eat whole grain products without a lot of sugar.

To really fill up your stomach until the next meal, go for protein servings (meat, chicken, fish, eggs, and dried beans) with good fats, like avocados and olive oil. A little dairy is okay too, but make it unsweetened yogurt or a slice of cheese, not ice cream.

Having a lot of fiber in your diet will also fill you up and improve your digestive motility as well. In addition to the aforementioned whole grains, try fresh fruits and vegetables. Leafy greens, broccoli, berries, and apples with the skin on, for example, are all high in fiber.

Use Journaling and Food Logging

While obsessing too much about your food can have a negative effect, if you have no idea how much food you're eating or if you want to improve your diet's nutritional content, think about keeping a food log. It doesn't have to be fancy or scientific; a simple list of what you eat and when you chow down can be very informative.

To add even more information, make a note about your mood that day or anything else that makes you feel like bingeing. You may find patterns you never knew existed, like every time your boss is in the office you overeat, or when your cousin calls, you always feel depressed afterward.

The key to learning from your journal is to look for patterns and be honest. If you didn't eat that bag of chips but you smoked half a pack of cigarettes instead, write that down. If you wanted to eat a trigger food but didn't, make a note of that too. It's important to keep track of your victories as you move forward.

Plan, Shop, and Prep for Meals in Advance

You can avoid a great deal of unplanned bingeing by having healthy alternatives at the ready instead. On Sunday or another day off, take a look at your schedule and plan out your meals for the week. Look at recipes for new ideas and try a different dish each week.

Once you know what you'll be eating, make a detailed shopping list and stick to it. Don't go to the grocery store on an empty stomach, or you're likely to fill your cart with stuff you don't need.

At home with your groceries, do a little advance prep work. Chop up fruits and vegetables for use throughout the week. Fix a few healthy meals and snacks ahead of time, so they're ready when you walk in the door at the end of an exhausting day. A few suggestions include:

- Hummus and vegetables.
- Cheese and fruit slices.
- Frozen mini quiches.

- Soup or chili.
- Mason jar salads (dressing, meat/cheese, veggies in layers- shake and serve).
- Stuffed peppers.
- Taco fixings.
- Spring rolls and dipping sauce.
- Casseroles in individual ramekins.
- Granola and dried fruit mixes.

Find New Activities to Replace Eating

Are you someone who likes to eat in front of the television or whenever friends come over? It could be you need to find something else to do with your hands while you're watching or visiting. If it's hard to just sit on the sofa and stare at the television, try knitting or crocheting during your TV time. Working with beads is another way to keep your hands busy, the back and forth stringing motion may satisfy the need to keep your hands moving without eating M&Ms, popcorn, or other trigger foods.

Other activities to replace eating that you can do alone or with others include:

- Giving yourself a manicure or pedicure.
- Refinishing or rehabbing small pieces of furniture.
- Arts and crafts, like origami or decoupage.
- Drawing and painting.
- Adult coloring books, a new craze. (https://www.cnn.com/2016/01/06/health/adult-coloring-books-popularity-mental-health/index.html)

- Scrapbooking.
- Sorting through old photos and papers.
- Folding laundry or ironing.
- Mending or hemming clothes.
- Potting plants or arranging flowers.
- Clipping recipes.
- Petting or grooming your animals.
- Making simple perfumes or personal care items with essential oils. https://www.immortalperfumes.com/sweet-tea-apothecary/2014/12/29/how-to-make-your-own-perfume-oil)
- Doing yoga stretches.
- Polishing jewelry or silverware.
- Writing holiday cards or thank-you notes.
- Rolling change to take to the bank.

Avoid Boredom

If you get bored in other situations, you can use the suggestions above, or you may need to get out of the house more. Many people binge eat simply because they have nothing better to do. Take a look at your daily calendar and see if there are empty spots you could fill with going for a walk, catching up on correspondence, visiting the library, or doing a home improvement project. Other options:

- Volunteer with a local charitable organization or your child's school.
- Plan the ultimate vacation.
- Join or start a club, like a book club.
- Take a class.

- Adopt a pet.
- Mentor someone at work.
- Go to local attractions, like historical sites, museums, zoos, and aquariums.
- Start a vegetable or flower garden.

Ask If You're Eating to Fill a Void

Some people eat because they feel an emptiness in their lives that goes beyond sheer boredom. Maybe it's because their family lives far away or they've just gone through a divorce. Perhaps becoming an empty nester or retiring leaves a void. If you find yourself eating to fill a hole in your life, you need to find a different solution.

While you can join groups or become more involved with other people, ultimately, your sense of fulfillment needs to come from within. Of course, it's fine to enjoy the company of others, but you want to be a whole person on your own.

If you find yourself unable to be alone for long, it could indicate you have issues that require attention beyond the scope of this book. Talk to a professional or have a chat with your religious leader to get to the root of this feeling and to develop self-sufficiency.

Eliminate Triggers

If boredom or lack of fulfillment are not causing your binge or emotional eating, there are other triggers that could be landmines in your attempts at healthy eating. As mentioned above, a journal or detailed food log can help expose triggers that cause you to overeat or to eat too much of certain foods.

Common triggers include stress, anxiety, depression, and fear. Sometimes certain people can send you running to the refrigerator. Maybe it's certain types of conversations, like talks that bring up unhappy memories or that make you feel confrontational.

If you have these triggers in your life, it's best to figure out how to remove them or, in the case of people you can't avoid, deal with them. Some suggestions for removing common disordered eating triggers are:

- Avoid people who spur binges whenever possible.
- Limit time with people who bring up unpleasant emotions.
- Change the topic if people bring up uncomfortable or depressing subjects.
- Don't put yourself in stressful situations (saying yes too often, running late, etc.)
- Script difficult conversations in advance.
- Use email if in-person conversation makes you flustered.
- Resist the urge to argue; instead, agree to disagree and let it go.
- Don't worry about things that haven't happened yet.
- Anticipate good outcomes rather than expecting the worst.

Find New Outlets for Your Feelings

Sometimes no matter what, you're going to have feelings that would have sent the "old" you diving into the pantry for a binge. But you can find other ways of channeling those feelings besides food, like:

- Punching a pillow or air boxing.
- Brisk walking or jogging.
- Swimming.
- Popping bubble paper.
- Hitting baseballs at the batting cages.
- Driving golf balls at the range.
- Yelling, singing, or chanting.
- Pranayama breathing. (https://www.youtube.com/watch?v=udLuhi5cktY)
- Dancing.
- Meditation and mindfulness practice.
- Housework or yard work, like sweeping, mowing the lawn, shoveling snow, or raking leaves.
- Take a bubble bath or go get a massage.

The idea isn't to suppress your emotions. It is to let them out in a way that doesn't involve eating. It's perfectly normal to have feelings, you don't want to drown them in junk food.

Reconsider Your Social Circle

There are certain people you may not be able to avoid, like your family, coworkers, or neighbors. However, there are indubitably people who may trigger unhappy emotions in you or even make you want to binge eat, and those people you can remove from your social life.

Do you have "friends" who make cutting remarks about your appearance or who always put others down? Do the people you hang out with make you feel low in other ways, maybe by their habits of wild partying or constant gossiping?

You may have to make peace with the idea that moving on in your life might mean leaving them behind, even if you feel a bit lonely for a while. But if you hang in there, you will make new, better friends, and you will find people who support your goal of a healthier life instead of dragging you down.

Create Healthy Routines

While your new routines are probably focused on eating better, if you create overall healthy routines, it will reinforce your plan to stop binge or emotional eating. For example, try to go to bed and get up at a regular time, and develop pleasant routines around these hours. Practice good sleep hygiene (http://healthysleep.med.harvard.edu/healthy/getting/overcoming/tips) and get up in time to fix a healthy breakfast instead of cramming down food in the car.

Make time for moderate exercise, meditation, or whatever else makes you feel good. Set time limits for other things you may tend to overdo in addition to eating, such as surfing social media or playing video games. Replace those activities with healthy food preparation and journaling, or another hobby entirely.

Don't Allow Yourself Cheat Days

One big mistake many binge eaters make is thinking they can have cheat days when they revert to their old overeating habits. This is not the same as allowing yourself one unhealthy snack while on a diet. You'll undo weeks of work with a big binge, and it may be enough to fall off the wagon completely.

Splurge on Non-Food Indulgences

If you feel the urge to splurge, try using something besides food to reward yourself. If you've lost weight by curbing binge eating, maybe it's time for some new clothes or to do something else for your appearance, like a haircut or makeup.

You can also treat yourself to new books, movie tickets, dance lessons, a beautiful leather-bound journal, or anything else that makes you feel good. If your normal impulse is to eat a bag of chips when you want to reward yourself after a tough week, ask yourself: what is it those chips make you feel? Then, find a reward that brings the same feeling, whether that's relief, power, or freedom. Instead of chips, get a facial, buy a new golf club, or go for a long drive in the country. You can find things that make you feel good that are not detrimental to your health.

Invest in Healthy Eating Tools

It's amazing what kind of cooking tools are on the market today. You can find a gadget or appliance for almost anything. Not only will these tools make your life easier, but some will also let you experiment with recipes you've never tried before.

Look at purchasing a few new kitchen goodies as an investment in healthy eating. Some items you may want to try:

- Reusable stretchy food wrappers for pineapple and melons.
- Avocado "huggers."
- Strawberry slicer.
- Clip-on pasta strainer.
- Specialty knives.
- Meatball molds.
- Tablet recipe stand.
- Toaster bags to make grilled sandwiches.
- Nesting food storage containers for take-out.
- Cutting board with a built-in food scale.
- Spiral vegetable slicer or mandoline.
- Silicone bread maker.
- Compartmentalized containers for salads, acai bowls, etc.
- Milk frother or immersion blender.
- Herb scissors and refrigerator keepers.
- Divided skillet to cook two foods separately at once.

Try Hypnosis

Hypnotherapy can be successful for some people in curing eating disorders. Hypnotherapy sessions usually start with a talk to discuss your problems and desired behavior. Then, the hypnotherapist uses relaxation techniques similar to a guided meditation to get you into a hypnotic state. You don't actually lose consciousness as you might see on television shows, but you will feel very "zoned out," like you're on the verge of sleep.

During the hypnotic state, the hypnotist usually introduces a post-hypnotic suggestion for you to act on once the session is over. You may be encouraged to eat more slowly, to pay better attention to hunger cues, or to replace a junk food binge favorite with something healthier, such as fruit or a salad.

Sometimes just one session does the trick. However, most people with eating disorders find a few sessions is better, either in a row or spread out for tweaking behavior after giving hypnosis an initial try.

If a hypnotherapist isn't in your budget, or if you're uncomfortable talking about your binge eating with a stranger, there are hypnotherapy CDs and audiobooks for eating disorders. Just like with meditation, you find a quiet spot and let the hypnotist guide you into better eating.

The biggest downside to DIY hypnosis is that you may need more time to go into a hypnotic state, which a live hypnotherapist can sense and provide on the fly during a session. With a CD or audiobook, obviously, you are dependent on reaching your hypnosis goals during the allotted time.

Use Essential Oils and Aromatherapy

Did you know there are essential oils you can use to help with binge eating? Certain scents help improve mood and can even curb appetite. If you're eating because you're depressed, or if you overeat because you don't receive normal cues to stop, you might want to give essential oils a try. Most essential oils should be used as aromatherapy- smelled, not ingested- but there are a few you can add to food.

The best essential oils for binge eating are:

- Cinnamon: reduces cravings, helps regulate blood sugar (can be consumed).
- Fennel: boosts metabolism, suppresses appetite, helps with sleep.
- Lavender: calms anxiety for emotional eaters.
- Rose: improves mood for depression-triggered bingers.
- Grapefruit: decreases food cravings and hunger pangs.

Always buy the highest grade essential oils you can, especially if you are ingesting them and not just enjoying their scent. For aromatherapy, you can make your own personal care products (there are a million how-to's online) or use them in a diffuser around the home. You can also combine oils according to your personal taste to make custom blends to reap multiple benefits in one fell swoop.

Learn to Listen to Hunger Cues

Some binge eaters acquired their eating disorder by failing to listen to the body's natural hunger cues over time until those cues became so blunted they stopped working. You'll notice that as you return to healthy eating patterns, those cues start to return. So, you want to pay extra attention to them this time around.

One way to develop a greater sensitivity to your body's messages about food is to slow down your eating. Even if you receive your hunger cues, they do no good if you've already eaten a box of cookies before they kick in.

Before having seconds or eating a large portion of anything, ask yourself, "Am I really hungry?" If the answer is no, put the rest away for another meal or take it to go from a restaurant (notorious for oversized portions). If you're not sure, take a few minutes' break from eating, sip some water, and then ask again. You may be surprised at how much you're eating when you're not even hungry anymore.

Have Compassion for Yourself

People with eating disorders tend to beat up on themselves extra hard, on top of the things that may be making them binge eat in the first place. Don't do this to yourself!

It's okay to run the gamut of human emotions. You just don't want to dwell on the negative ones or suppress them through food. If you're kind to yourself when you feel "negative" emotions, like sadness or anger, they will pass more quickly, and you're less likely to overeat as a reaction.

Give Up on Perfection

While you're at it, forget trying to be perfect. No one is, even the people you think are. Everyone has moments where they feel not up to snuff; it's just that some people are better at hiding it than others, and some people get over these feelings more quickly too.

One thing that doesn't help in this regard is social media. If seeing other people's "perfect" lives on Instagram and Facebook make you depressed or jealous, remember you're not seeing the entire picture, only what they want you to see. Take a break from social media if it makes you feel triggered; put the time into something more constructive.

If you are trying to lose weight after gaining some from an eating disorder, have patience with where you're at. Remind yourself of how far you've come, even if it's just psychologically, and look forward to putting more behind you with time. Know you will never reach perfection. Set aspirational but reachable goals and take as much time as you need to get there.

Get Rid of Gender Stereotypes

Don't feel like you need to "eat like a girl" or "devour food like a real man." These are stereotypes that society thrusts onto people and can affect your eating habits. You may be eating in secret because you believe women shouldn't eat anything but salads. Or you might be a guy who wants salads but feels pressure to eat meat and potatoes. Eat what you like, and too bad what others say!

Let Go of a Scarcity Mindset

Did your binge eating develop as the result of food scarcity somewhere in your past? It's possible you overeat now because you experienced food insecurity as a child or even went through periods as an adult where you felt there wasn't enough food.

As long as you have sufficient food now, you can let that mindset go. And if you don't have enough food, consult with your local resources or area food bank to get what you need.

Remind yourself you have plenty of food; say it out loud or put messages on the fridge if you have to. At a party and feel like you need to have three pieces of cake? Tell yourself there will be other opportunities for delicious treats, and savor one slice instead of bingeing. If the feeling of scarcity persists, it may be time to talk with a professional.

Pay Attention to Actual Food Needs

There are cravings and then there are food needs. It's perfectly okay to feel like you need more unrefined carbohydrates for natural energy or protein to keep your blood sugar more stable. If you're exercising, especially in hot weather, you may need salt to replace the sodium chloride lost in sweat.

When you feel the urge to eat something particular, examine the craving. Is it something healthy you want? Is there a logical and sound reason behind it? Then go ahead and indulge with moderation. If your cravings involve junk or refined food, watch out. You may be caving into a bingeing urge, in which case you should consider if there is something healthier you could be eating.

Don't Punish and Reward Your Kids With Food

If you have children, never use food to reward or punish them. This only reinforces the dysfunctional ideas you have about eating, and it could create another generation of eating disorders.

Instead of using food as a prize, make it just an ordinary part of your day. Enjoy it, appreciate its nutrition, and use something else to reward your kids, like extra TV time or a new game. By telling your kids about healthy food philosophies, you are reiterating good thoughts like a little mantra.

Understand Binge Eating Is on a Spectrum

There is an enormous range of problems on the continuum of eating disorders, from people who occasionally overindulge, to people who overeat every day and even purge the contents of their stomachs. If you fall into the latter category, it's best to seek help from a medical professional because the consequences of purging can be life-threatening.

However, if you fall lower on the eating disorder spectrum, you may be wondering about things like whether you should totally forbid yourself certain types of food or if you can eat "just one donut." Only you will know the answer to those questions, but you could consider approaching the situation like someone with an addiction.

If you feel like trying one donut would result in you eating the entire box, it's best to keep them off your menu entirely. On the other hand, if you don't normally go overboard with a taste of something, you may be able to eat it in small quantities. Just limit how much you have access to at any point in time. For some people, knowing they don't need to completely deprive themselves of a food makes it easier to stay in control.

It may take some experimentation to determine your personal willpower when it comes to trigger foods. And your behavior may change over time as you have more success living without certain foods. Think about a song or a video game you were obsessed with years ago. You can probably hear or play them now without any risk of going back to being "addicted" to them because you've gained maturity and perspective.

Eat in Stages

One strategy some former binge eaters have employed when testing the waters with trigger foods is to eat in stages. Buy one donut, for example, and say, "This is my one donut for the week. I'm not going to have another one until next week."

You can apply this stage strategy to all of your meals. "I'm going to have one serving of chicken, and then I'm going to wait 10 minutes. If I'm still hungry then, I'll decide about having another helping."

Put some barriers between foods you feel worried about eating too much of. Rather than baking two potatoes, bake one. If you really, really, really feel you need the second one, you're going to have to wait for it to cook before you can have it. Buy single-serving portions of "danger" foods whenever possible. Or as soon as you get home from the store, divide up big packages into small containers and freeze them- whatever you have to do to slow down your eating and make you think before indulging too much.

Measure and Weigh Your Food

While earlier you read that dieting can actually derail a plan to stop binge eating, you may have to use some tools of the crafty dieter. This is especially true if you have a tendency to underestimate how much you're eating or if you prepare gigantic servings without thinking.

Get a food scale and some measuring cups, so you can know how much you're actually consuming. You may think you're eating one serving of a food when you are really eating two or more. If you're used to eating in restaurants, you may be particularly spoiled by extra large portions that could be divided into several meals.

Remember the "eating in stages" strategy? You can do that when you eat out too. Simply take half the food on your plate and set it aside. If you're still hungry after you eat the first half and wait 10 minutes or more, you can have it (or maybe divide that portion in half again). Better yet, put half the meal directly into a to-go container to bring it home with you.

Improve the Quality of Your Meals

Are your meals haphazard affairs eaten standing at the kitchen counter or in the car? That is no way to encourage healthy eating habits.

Take a page from people in many other countries outside of the United States, and prepare your dining ambiance for savoring your food. Lay a tablecloth (or use colorful placemats if you have kids), set out some candles, use your good china, and put on some music for dinner. Even if you eat on your own, you can do this.

Eliminate distractions, like television, while you're eating or checking your cell phone every few minutes. The idea is to focus on the meal and what you're eating, so you eat more slowly and make the meal an enjoyable event, not a pie-eating contest.

It can be challenging to do this every night if you have kids with busy after-school activities or a spouse who comes home late. Even if you do it once or twice a week, your family may like it so much that they make an effort to have a special meal more often. If you involve the kids in planning and setting the table, that may draw them in too.

Never Eat Out of the Container

It goes without saying that if you're eating at the dining room table in a civilized way, then you're not eating directly out of take-out cartons or plastic bags. One of the easiest ways to accidentally binge eat is to eat out of a container.

Always take your food out of the container and put it in a bowl or on a plate. Resist the urge to drink juice straight from the bottle or eat ice cream out of the tub. You'll have a better idea of how much you're eating if you serve it first, and it makes you appreciate the food more.

Take a look at the size of your plates and bowls too. Consider using smaller vessels for your food. It will look like more, and you'll be less likely to eat restaurant-size portions. As a bonus, cleanup will be easier, and you can run your dishwasher less often.

You don't have to make this a sad experience. Even at a thrift or dollar store, you can find cute small dishes and antique glasses. Or try a Japanese bento box that limits serving sizes to the dimensions of each little compartment. Look for bento boxes that are similar to those used in Japanese restaurants- a bit like a TV dinner tray- rather than the ones the function as lunchboxes for kids, unless you also want to take your meals to work or school.

Try EFT/Tapping

Tapping, also known as EFT (the Emotional Freedom Technique https://youtu.be/QzVd6Ww0as4) is a relatively new way to quell unwanted behavior, from binge eating and smoking to worry and angry outbursts. It uses concepts from modern-day psychology with Ancient Chinese acupressure to communicate directly with parts of the brain associated with stress and emotion, bypassing the thinking part of the brain and going straight to the amygdala where fight-or-flight responses are processed.

You start by tapping your fingers on meridian points of the body- places where energy concentrates- while reciting statements about the problem you want to solve. For binge eating or emotional eating, you might say as your set-up statement for the first meridian point, "Even though I sometimes eat too much to hide my feelings, I accept and love myself."

Then, as you move through the other points, you state how you feel, for example, "I feel embarrassed about my eating habits." It's okay if you feel like you're venting. The idea is to clear the energy around whatever is bothering you and start to feel better. You want to do a few rounds of this at least once per day to help clear old emotions and make room for healthier living.

Remarkably, these tapping techniques have been used by many people for great relief and improvement in their mental health. It's particularly effective for PTSD (post-traumatic stress disorder), anxiety, depression, and addiction. The great thing about learning about tapping for disordered eating is that you can use it for other problems in your life that have nothing to do with diet or weight.

Use Mental Imagery and Visualization

For some people, harnessing the power of the mind is a great way to help them achieve healthier eating habits. One way to use your imagination is to picture yourself sitting down to a delicious meal at a nice table involving appropriate portions of healthy food.

Close your eyes and visualize what the food looks, smells, and tastes like. See yourself through your own eyes, eating slowly, putting down your fork when you've had enough, and sipping water to break up your eating. You can imagine yourself at home doing this or with your family or at your favorite restaurant.

You can also create vision boards with images of your desired eating habits, meals, and table settings. If you're the crafty type, grab a stack of magazines and catalogs and make a collage to hang on your fridge or tuck in your mirror. You can snap a picture of it with your phone to take with you when you need a little extra willpower.

Another option is to use Pinterest and create a digital board to inspire you. You can select from millions of images other users have already pinned on the site using their search function, and you can upload your own images from your phone or from the web.

You'll find excellent recipes there too, as well as wellness infographics, table decor (https://www.pinterest.com/search/pins/?q=table%20setting s&rs=typed&term_meta[]=table%7Ctyped&term_meta[]=s ettings%7Ctyped), and exercise gear. In addition to creating a board for eating habits (which you can make secret, by the way, if you don't want anyone else to see it), you could make one each for yoga poses, cool kitchen gadgets, single-serving recipes, and most inspirational quotes.

Engage in Positive Self-Talk and Affirmations

One behavior many binge and emotional eaters have in common is negative self-talk. This won't help you break bad habits, and it reinforces beliefs about yourself that you want to get rid of. To get rid of this unproductive pattern, try catching yourself any time you say something negative, like "I'm terrible at controlling myself around food," or "My life stinks."

You don't have to go on about unicorns and rainbows; it's enough to pivot slightly from the negative talk to something more positive in a general direction. For example, replace "I'm so bad in social situations" with "I do better in small groups where I can talk to people one on one." Instead of "I'll never lose any weight," say, "As I learn to control my eating, the weight will come off and stay off. I'm in the process of developing healthy habits."

Affirmations (statements of belief) like "I'm so skinny," or "I have mastered healthy choices," may not sound convincing if those things are not true. If you desire something but haven't achieved it yet, try using the phrase "I'm in the process of" when creating your own affirmations. It will ring truer with you, and therefore the affirmation will be more effective.

You can write your healthy eating affirmations (https://motivationalhypnotherapy.com/streaming/meditations-for-healthy-eating/) on your mobile phone, on index cards, or anywhere else you'll see them regularly. A good idea is to go through your affirmations- maybe a half dozen or so- first thing in the morning and again right before sleep at night. You can even create beautiful affirmation cards on free design platforms like Canva, where you select a layout, drop in photos you like, and write your own inspirational text.

Pay Attention to Dopamine Hits

Did you know your body has a reward center (https://www.ncbi.nlm.nih.gov/pmc/articles/PMC3368677/) that pays out like a Las Vegas slot machine when you engage in certain activities? It is now understood that the body releases dopamine, a neurotransmitter used in the brain when you engage in certain activities that feel good to you. This includes shopping, gaming, using drugs, and overeating.

Do you have certain habits that feel almost compulsive to you? The more you engage in a pleasurable activity, the more you may crave doing it again, all thanks to dopamine hits that make your brain happy.

The good news is you can retrain your brain over time to get pleasure from something besides binge eating or any other habit that's not good for you in the long run. Watch for conditions (triggers) that predispose you to repeat the same undesirable behavior. The first step is to look for clues to your dopamine-induced overeating. Maybe you eat too much every time you turn on the television or every time your coworker makes a biting remark.

Next, you want to replace the unwanted behavior that follows the trigger with something more desirable. For example, if you are tempted to open a bag of chips every time you get your evening's entertainment, think of what you could do instead, like yoga asanas, hopping on the treadmill, or folding the laundry. Eventually, your brain will start to associate the trigger with a new activity, and you'll be weaning yourself off those dopamine infusions for binge eating.

Have Tricks Up Your Sleeve When You Can't Resist Eating

There will be times along the road to wellness when you will still want to binge eat or hide your emotions in food. It's wise in this case to have a few tricks you can rely on at the last minute to keep from eating when you know you shouldn't but your willpower is fading:

- Give the food to someone else quickly or toss it in the trash or garbage disposal.
- Put the food in the freezer.
- Brush your teeth, so nothing tastes good.
- Eat a eucalyptus cough drop to make food taste even worse.
- Pop a stick of strong-flavored chewing gum.
- Eat a breath mint or powerful mouthwash strip.
- Apply some dental whitening strips or trays.
- Wear boxing gloves, so you can't eat with your hands.

- Think about something unappetizing to put you off your food.
- Get in the car and go someplace.
- Go out for a walk.

Get Help from Professionals

If you find yourself overwhelmed by your binge eating or emotional eating, it may be time to consult a professional. There's no stigma in asking for help, and you may not need it long term, only for a while until you can go it on your own.

According to the National Eating Disorders Association, there are signs that you need to seek medical help right away. These include:

- Developing behaviors associated with anorexia nervosa (sudden weight loss, not eating at all, cessation of menstrual periods, etc.).
- Purging after eating (making yourself vomit).
- Using laxatives to undo the effects of binge eating.
- Health problems related to poor diet or binge-purge cycles.
- Feeling "fat" even after you have lost a significant amount of weight.

If you think you need medical attention, it's better to err on the side of caution and see a doctor than to ignore your symptoms. While this book can help cure binge eating and emotional eating, some cases need professional interference.

There are different types of professionals who deal with eating disorders. General practitioners, like family doctors, can sometimes recognize eating disorder signs, but they usually refer those patients to a clinic specializing in disordered eating. Those clinics usually combine medical treatment with talk therapy for the best results.

Both psychologists and psychiatrists can provide talk therapy, but it's typically the former who schedules those sessions, while psychiatrists prescribe medications and deal with things requiring a medical degree.

You may also want to consult with a dietary consultant, like a nutritionist or a dietician. A dietician generally has more credentials than a nutritionist, having completed an internship, while there are fewer formal requirements to be a nutritionist. Your primary care provider can probably recommend a practitioner to help with your diet if you do not know how to eat healthily or where to get various nutrients.

Climb Back in the Saddle When You Fall off the Horse

As you work towards more healthy eating, it's quite possible you will have setbacks. You may binge eat or resort to emotional eating during periods of stress. While you can have the best of intentions to control your eating habits, life can throw unexpected events at you, such as family illness, job loss, or relationship breakups.

What's important is that you don't give up when these disappointments happen. Everybody regresses somehow when confronted by life's biggest challenges. See them as blips on the radar screen of life and then go back to working on healthy eating.

Chapter Summary

This chapter offered different ways to curb emotional and binge eating.

- No one method may be perfect for you; you can also use them in combination.
- These methods may change as your healthy eating improves and you need to tweak your current strategies.
- If you have a setback and resort to binge eating or eating emotionally, don't let that derail your progress. Instead, get right back to your healthy eating plan.

In the next chapter, you will learn several tips on how to prevent a relapse.

Chapter Five: Tips On How To Prevent A Relapse

After discussing the methods you can use to treat emotional eating and binge eating in the previous chapter, it important to discuss tips that will help prevent a relapse. Learning how to prevent a relapse into your old unhealthy eating habits makes it easy for you to follow through with treatment. In this chapter, we will discuss several tips that will help you successfully transition from unhealthy eating habits to healthy ones.

Tips to prevent a relapse

The truth of the matter is recovering from binge eating and emotional eating will not be a walk in the park. It will take effort, time, and persistence to ensure that you get over binge eating and emotional eating disorder and get back control over food. Below are tips that will help prevent a relapse as well as give you the motivation to keep moving forward despite the challenges you face.

1. Have a plan

While still on treatment, it is essential to have a plan that will keep you from reverting to your old unhealthy eating habits. The plan can include a food journal and a meal plan. Having a plan is important for the following reasons:

It helps you track your progress: Having a plan while on treatment for an eating disorder like binge eating helps you track your progress. For instance, having a food journal will help you understand the number of calories you eat daily. It will also make it possible to portion your meals and include healthy snacks. Having a method that makes it easy to track your progress helps you know when you experience a relapse.

It enables you to achieve your objectives: One of the most significant objectives of a plan is enabling you to achieve your objectives. Every individual with an eating disorder has a set of objectives they want to achieve. It does, however, become quite difficult to stick to the objectives they set. However, having a plan is a constant reminder that there is a reason to keep working and sticking to the treatment.

It motivates you to keep going: An excellent plan will have incentives that will make it possible for you to keep working to achieve your objectives. It should motivate you and keep you from losing track even when faced with challenges. Having a plan will motivate you to make the right decisions even when you feel like making all the wrong choices.

How to Create a Plan

When creating a plan, it is essential to ask yourself the following questions.

- How will your diet plan look? The answer to this question depends on the schedule your treatment plan has for you. You should also consider the number of meals you desire to eat in a day. Having an eating schedule will make it easy for you to divide calories accordingly and eliminate the possibility of overindulging.
- What type of support do you require? Your support system is also necessary to include in your plan. Having support while trying to succeed in getting back your self-control over food helps you stick to your nutrition and treatment plans without falling off the wagon.
- Do you require exercise? This another aspect to consider. However, before you include it as part of your routine, it is important for you to consult your doctor. Becoming physically active makes it easy to lose weight as well as give your body the energy it requires to keep going.

2. Do not skip your meals

Plenty of relapses among individuals suffering from binge eating and emotional eating disorders happen because of skipping a meal. To avoid relapsing, it is essential to never let yourself get extremely hungry. Extreme hunger will make you overeat during one sitting and this may lead to you resorting to your unhealthy habits. For people suffering from binge eating and emotional eating disorders, skipping meals will not help you manage this condition.

Skipping meals also have serious effects on people with eating disorders. It affects you physically and mentally as well. The physical effects of skipping meals include increased glucose and sugar levels, abdominal weight gain, and overeating. Psychologically, skipping meals will cause a drastic change in your mood. In chapter three, we discussed the relationship between food and your emotions. Thus, the more you skip meals, the more emotional you become. Here are some tips that will keep you from skipping meals:

Have a reminder: Being constantly told by society that eating regularly is bad and not eating is good, it is easy to believe that to be true. However, you are actually much better off eating all your meals rather than skipping them. Having a reminder is one of the ways to ensure you never skip a meal. Eating all your meals is important as it helps you stick to your treatment plans without having a reason to binge eat.

Always plan ahead: We all have those days when our lives are constantly stressful and during those moments, it becomes quite easy to turn to food to lift your spirit. This can eventually lead to a relapse. Planning your meals is one way of avoiding a relapse. Once you plan your snacks and prep your meals beforehand, it takes away any excuses you give yourself to eat food that may cause you to relapse.

Talk to your doctor: If you cannot stop yourself from skipping meals talk to your doctor or a therapist. They will help you come up with effective ways to ensure you eat healthier and regularly.

Eating on a regular basis will help control your hunger, avoid situations that can lead to bingeing sessions, and it stops you from feeling hungry. Remember, skipping meals can trigger emotional or binge eating symptoms and this can derail your recovery process.

3. Occasionally treat yourself

Treating yourself occasionally is one way to ensure that you stick to your objectives without diverting attention to unhealthy foods. Individuals suffering from binge eating disorder or emotional eating disorder have to divide the food they consume into two categories. The "good" category or the "risky" category. Dividing food in such a manner makes it easy for you to avoid including the risky foods as part of your daily meals.

However, such a division can cause you to have a relapse. One of the ways to avoid this is by occasionally treating yourself. Why is it important to treat yourself?

- It helps you remain motivated

According to several research studies, occasionally treating yourself can assist you in staying motivated. Creating specific goals for yourself during your treatment journey and then ensuring that you treat yourself after achieving it, helps you stay motivated to achieve a holistic and healthy approach in dealing with your triggers and emotions. In order for you to attain optimal results, ensure that you break down your long-term goals into shorter and more achievable goals. This will make it possible for you to reward yourself when you accomplish the shorter goals.

- It prevents a decrease in your metabolic rate

Another benefit of occasionally rewarding yourself is that it helps in preventing a decrease in your metabolic rate. One of the action treatment plans for people suffering from binge eating disorder or emotional eating disorder is the creation of a meal plan. A majority of foods on meal plans are healthy foods. However, completely eradicating some food types can cause your body to experience a decrease in its metabolic rate. The primary reason for this is because your metabolism (the part of your body responsible for digesting food and helps in its storage and excretion) recognizes the food you consume.

This causes your body to decrease the work your metabolism performs and this may result in you gaining even more weight. For this reason, I do not recommend completely cutting out an entire food group. For example, if you were to try a diet (which isn't right for everyone), something that says low-carb may be fine but be wary of something that says no-carb as completely removing foods can lower your metabolic rate. This is also why occasionally treating yourself will not only make it easy for you to lose weight; it also prevents occasional cravings.

- It keeps you from binge eating

Finally, treating yourself from time to time prevents you from falling into a binge episode. Categorizing specific foods as bad is one of the primary reasons why people relapse when undergoing treatment for an eating disorder.

Research has found that people who crave specific foods and end up preventing themselves from eating them, will end up experiencing emotional eating or bingeing episodes.

This is because people who crave for specific foods will opt for healthier options and since this will not satisfy their cravings, they end up eating, even more, to attempt to satisfy their craving. However, this would not be the case if they had simply eaten the food their bodies craved for. Therefore, occasionally treating yourself is an effective method of ensuring you stick to your treatment and avoid bingeing episodes.

Remember, your objective should be to incorporate a wide range of food varieties and eat them in moderation.

4. Stay positive

It is important to remember that there are plenty of challenges when undergoing treatment for binge eating disorder and emotional eating. One of the most common challenges is failing to follow through with the treatment and having to start all over again. Having treated binge eating before, I know how it feels to relapse back to binge eating and have to start treatment all over again. Despite it being tough, staying positive about your success, body shape, and yourself, helps you get through the difficult times. What makes positivity a powerful weapon when undergoing treatment for eating disorders?

First, it is important to understand that positivity plays a significant role in your treatment process. Negative thoughts lead to self-defeating actions like overeating, turning to food for comfort, and going off your treatment and nutrition plan. Positive thoughts are empowering and they help you through the entire process of recovery. Berating yourself any time you fail to do something right, focusing on what you did not do, or dreading your meals can lead to you relapsing and going back to unhealthy eating habits.

Secondly, positivity helps you stick to your goals despite the challenges you face. It makes it easy for you to have an attitude that forces you to achieve success despite the challenges you face along the way. Your society, family, or environment cannot influence your attitude. Therefore, strive to have an attitude that will help you stick to your treatment and nutrition despite the challenges you face.

5. Ensure you have a support system

It is hard to ignore the fact that trying to recover from an eating disorder has its difficulties and successes. During each stage of your treatment having people you can depend on during the difficult and challenging times makes the treatment easier to cope with. You need people who understand the struggles you go through. You require people who will listen to your fears and offer you an honest opinion on what you should do during the difficult times.

Research studies have shown that people with support systems have better-coping skills, high levels of well-being, and healthier lives. Research also shows that having a support system helps in reducing depression and anxiety. Anxiety and depression are some emotions that can lead individuals recovering from binge eating disorder or emotional eating disorder into a relapse. To prevent this from happening, it is essential to have a support system.

Types of support systems

The primary objective of any support system is to reduce the amount of stress you may experience when undergoing the treatment process. Support systems are classified into four categories. These four categories are:

Esteem support: This is a type of support that is expressed in the form of encouragement or confidence. People in your life offering esteem support point out the strengths you overlook when you feel down or unable to complete the treatment. This type of support inspires confidence in yourself due to the amount of confidence your support system offers you. Esteem social support also leads to you believing that you can accomplish anything once you put your mind to it.

Emotional support: This is the type of support that comprises physical comfort like constant pats on the back, hugs, empathizing, or simply listening. Emotional support helps you receive big hugs, listening ears, and advice from friends, family, and people who understand what you are going through. You can also receive emotional support from a group of people undergoing the same treatment or people who have succeeded in curing binge eating disorder or emotional eating. Listening to advice from people who have been through the same experiences as yourself, makes it easy for you to continue with the treatment despite the odds.

Tangible support: Tangible support involves taking on certain responsibilities for somebody else to help them deal with problems they are experiencing. In other words, tangible support is simply taking an active role in helping someone deal with the challenges they are dealing with when undergoing treatment. For instance, your family can help you prep your meals to avoid eating unhealthy foods that can result in a relapse.

Informational support: Informational support is simply offering advice, gathering information, and sharing the results based on what an individual requires. This type of support is essential as it helps you learn what to do every step of the way. For individuals recovering from an eating disorder, your informational support should always be your doctor or therapist.

Remember; always be honest with your support network as this will help make your journey easy and more achievable.

6. Manage your triggers

When trying to cure an eating disorder it is important to set yourself up for an accomplishment by ensuring you do not expose yourself to unhealthy foods that can cause you to relapse. The first step in accomplishing this is by knowing your triggers. Identifying your triggers is a necessary requirement for individuals undergoing treatment for eating disorders. How do you identify your triggers?

- Start by examining your eating habits. When examining your eating habits ensure that you identify the feelings that cause you to eat even when you are not hungry. Once you recognize those feelings, it is important to try to identify the emotion you are trying to create or avoid with food.

- Take a pen and a piece of paper and record each of the emotions you are trying to create or avoid. Documenting each of these emotions makes it easy to identify when your turn to food to create an emotion or avoid it.

- Next, try to recall what happened the last time you experienced a bingeing episode or tried to eat your emotions. Recalling the emotions you experienced enables you to learn what causes you to emotionally eat. It also helps you identify when you are most vulnerable to relapses.

- On that piece of paper, create two columns. The first column is an emotions column while the second one is a response column. In the first column, try to identify the emotions that cause a trigger reaction to food. On the second column, try to write down the responses you have to the emotions you experience. For instance, perhaps you got angry and your immediate response to this emotion was eating a large bag of chips. Whatever your response was, ensure that you note it down.

- If you have responses that are repetitive, then now you know what triggers cause you to binge eat or eat your emotions.

How do You Manage Your Triggers?

As I mentioned earlier, recognizing your triggers is the first step in managing your triggers. Identifying your triggers helps you learn various ways to help you cope with them rather than turn to food for solace. You can do this by incorporating activities you enjoy doing, or talking to a therapist to deal with your various issues.

- Accept your feeling even the negative ones. This will help you feel more and learn how to deal with these emotions.
- Keeping a food journal is another way that can help you manage your triggers. A food diary will help you keep track of what you eat when you eat, the amount of food you consume, and why you eat. This will enable you to separate your emotional hunger from your physical hunger and recognize when your unhealthy eating habits are starting up again.
- Try to practice mindful eating. This is possible by eating with no distractions, as this will help you appreciate your food, its taste, and smell. You should also take smaller bites and eat slowly as this will help you feel fuller.
- Make sure you re-organize your environment to keep you from overeating, like meal planning, having healthy snacks on hand to avoid eating unhealthy snacks, and portion control.

- Listening to your body can also help you develop awareness of your satiety and hunger cues.
- Try to incorporate exercise as part of your daily routine. Exercise will help keep you distracted from the negative emotions. It will also help boost your confidence.
- Also, ensure that your diets are well balanced, as this will help reduce your cravings and re-balance your body's functionality.
- Ensure that you keep unhealthy foods out of your fridge and pantry. This will keep you from a relapse.

7. Seek professional help

I understand how scary it is to realize that you no longer have control over your eating habits despite following the treatment to the letter. However, it is essential to remember that the help you require to get back on the right path is just an email or phone call away. Seeking professional help is important as it helps you deal with the relapse. It also increases your likelihood of recovering from an eating disorder. There is a variety of help available for you from professionals. They are always around to help you recover as well as get back up from a relapse.

How to Recognize When You Require Professional Help

Relapse includes mental and behavior changes, which cause one to revert back to unhealthy eating habits. It can also include thoughts that focus too much on your weight, diet or counting calories. This can cause you to excessively worry about a loss of self-control. It is important to understand that there is a high likelihood for people who have struggled with eating disorders for a long time to have numerous relapses.

Another aspect to consider when it comes eating disorder relapses is that your relapse rate will vary depending on the treatment you receive, your age, your interpersonal interactions, and your eating disorder habits. Relapsing does not mean that you have failed in binge eating or emotional eating recovery. It is simply a step that helps you learn how to cope with the numerous challenges you face on the road to recovery. Always remember, that you will get through a relapse. Seeking professional advice enables you to acquire the help you so badly need.

What Type of Treatment do you Require?

The one question people ask quite a lot is what type of professional help should I look for. Should I go to a therapist? Or should visit my doctor? The answers to these questions depend on the nature of your relapses. For instance, if you relapsed due to the amount of pressure you have from friends, family and your environment, then it would be wise to visit a therapist to help you deal with these issues.

If your relapse was due to a lack of a specific food in your meal, then talking to your doctor is the best approach to take. Your doctor will help you come up with an inclusive meal plan. This makes it possible to avoid unhealthy foods and manage your cravings.

8. Strive for consistency and not perfection

When recovering from an eating disorder it is essential to realize that, it will take months for you to stop emotional eating or binge eating habits. Your recovery will require work and effort. Changing your eating behaviors is not going to happen overnight but with consistency, it becomes easier to practice. Hence, striving for consistency and not perfection helps in ensuring you do not relapse. People who strive for perfection try to ensure they do not slip-up along the way and this increases room for failure. While people who strive for consistency, understand that there will be slip-ups along the way, but they do not allow their failures to define their recovery. Here are a few tips to help you remain consistent:

Start slowly and gradually progress: A majority of people make the mistake of beginning their recovery process with a high intensity and this may make it impossible for them to keep up after some time. Changing your diet and unhealthy eating habits within a single day or one week is something impossible to do and very unhelpful. Therefore, it is essential for you to start by changing one aspect at a time and then gradually increasing the changes.

Accountability: It is quite easy to relapse back to your previous unhealthy eating habits when you have no one to hold you accountable. You may end up eating that bar of chocolate simply because no one will reprimand you for making that choice. However, feeding your cravings when trying to recover from binge eating disorder will cause you to derail your treatment. Having an accountability partner will help you stick to your treatment and nutrition plan and work hard to recover from binge eating disorder or emotional eating.

Do not depend on motivation: Motivation is important, but it is short lived especially when undergoing months of treatment for an eating disorder. After weeks of being motivated to stick to your treatment, you may start feeling de-motivated and this can cause you to relapse. Therefore, to prevent a relapse from happening, make healthy eating habits a constant practice. The more you stick to your treatment and nutrition plan, the easier it becomes to do it even without motivation.

Develop small habits: Developing habits that seem insignificant when treating an eating disorder is an essential part of being consistent with your treatment. Some of these small habits include drinking eight glasses of water on a daily basis, avoiding junk food, and exercising for at least 30 minutes daily, among others. Developing these habits is difficult at first but it ends up becoming easier with regular practice.

Set and achieve short-term goals: Recovering from an eating disorder often takes months to accomplish. Therefore, setting short-term goals that will help make your recovery process go smoothly, you'll be able to accomplish each goal without having to worry about the long-term goals. You can also set-up a reward system (that does not include food) that allows you to reward yourself once you achieve a certain short-term goal.

Relapses are part of your treatment journey- do not give up even when you experience a backslide. You have what it takes to stick to your recovery process. With the above tips, you can achieve the success you want and prevent relapses from occurring.

Chapter Summary

- Learning how to prevent a relapse into your old unhealthy eating habits makes it easy for you to follow through with treatment.
- Some ways to avoid a relapse is through having a plan, acquiring support, not skipping meals, and being positive.

Final Words

After learning and discussing binge eating and emotional eating in-depth, I hope it has helped to shed light on the various changes you can make to recover from an eating disorder. I hope you understand that binge eating episodes or emotional eating are not your fault and that you do require help to recover and regain control of food once more.

Recovering from an eating disorder will definitely take time but the end results are absolutely worth it. I understand how tough the journey may be, but with support from friends and family, you will definitely recover and regain control of your health and eating habits once more. Remember, your recovery starts with you and you have the power to transform your life as long as you take the necessary steps to get there.

If you enjoyed and found this book valuable, please leave a short review on Amazon!

55017854R00083

Made in the USA
Columbia, SC
08 April 2019